MERRITT LIBRARY
1018451095
641.8653 SMI
Smith, Janet
Cupcakes / Janet Smith :
photographs by Deirdre Roon

JUN 17 2009

WITHDRAWN

Cupcakes

D1476382

Janet Smith

Photographs by Deirdre Rooney

Cupcakes

Thompson-Nicola Regional District
Library System
300-465 VICTORIA STREET
KAMLOOPS, BC   V2C 2A9

whitecap

1018451095

AAhhh cupcakes, they are so gorgeous! There is just something about a cute little cake baked in its own paper case that is irresistible. Baking cupcakes is not fraught with the stresses of other kinds of baking, and they give immediate gratification on so many levels.

Fulfill artistic urges with the millions of combinations of toppings and cake mixes and change them to go with moods and fashions. I definitely like to keep my colour schemes in tune with what's happening on the catwalk. If you're feeling dampened by a dull rainy day, wile away the afternoon and lift your spirits with a batch of sweet little cakes, toast some crumpets, get out your prettiest cups and linens and you will be in heaven – if you can add an open fire, a pretty shaggy dog and a handsome rugged man to the mix, so much the better.

Remember those sad days when cupcakes were saved for children's birthdays and afternoon tea? Not anymore: now, they can be served after dinner and at weddings and also appear at premieres and cocktail parties everywhere.

The most basic recipe can be topped and dressed to look fabulous by the most inexperienced cook and, as long as you use quality basic ingredients, they will taste fantastic too.

I try to combine my love of cupcakes with my love of fashion and styling. Afternoon tea is the perfect occasion for indulging yourself in dressing up and fashion fantasies. There's traditional tea that requires vintage tea dresses, sparkly sandals and fresh flowers with cupcakes served on classic mismatched china with soft embroidered linens. For cutting-edge tea, think smart boutique hotel or New York loft. This requires an altogether different look: we're talking perfectly manicured fingernails, giant cocktail rings and designer dresses. Vivienne Westwood is good to add a slightly mad hatter feel – vertiginous heels essential. Cupcakes are served on smart white china with crisp pressed napkins and Champagne, not tea, is my drink of choice on this occasion.

And let's not forget all the cupcake (not fashion) styling and shopping opportunities. For presents and parties trawl the shops (or the Internet if you prefer) for pretty wrappings, papers and boxes (I have become slightly obsessive about saving boutique packaging). It's possible to waste hours wandering about charity shops and flea markets looking for quirky teacups and saucers, retro cake stands and elegant napkins. And don't forget all the chocolatiers and delicatessens in the world – you get travel opportunities with cupcakes as well. They must be visited at every opportunity for inspiration and sources of interesting paper cases, sprinkles, dragées and sweets (hard to beat a unique travel-sourced decoration or wrapping) and unusually flavoured chocolate.

Having made all these wonderful creations, get out your camera and take some snapshots, keep them in a scrapbook and you have a beautiful art collection as well. Enjoy.

Equipment and ingredients

Equipment and ingredients

Equipment

A good set of scales

Essential, obviously. I like to use electronic weigh-and-go style scales as the ingredients for all-in-one mixes can be weighed in the mixing bowl – also saves on washing up.

Wooden spoons

Try to keep a selection just for cake-making. You don't want your buttercream tasting of garlic or onions.

Spatula

A lovely, bendy flexible spatula makes it easy to get at every last scrap of cake mixture.

Measuring spoons

A set of these is useful for measuring small quantities of raising agent.

A good, sharp grater

Essential for removing zest from citrus fruit. If your grater is blunt, throw it away.

Tins and cases

These come in so many shapes and sizes, and all are labelled differently, so it's hard to be really specific and exact. Be guided by the recipes but don't overfill the cases or the mixture will leak out everywhere and your cakes will not look pretty. You can also make cupcakes without a special tin – just put them on a baking tray – but they will not stay a nice regular shape. Some very moist cupcakes are best cooked in sturdy foil cases as they keep their shape better.

A 12-hole cupcake tin is a regular cupcake tin and the indentations are quite shallow. This tin is used for regular-size cupcake cases. A muffin tin will also have 12 holes, but the indentations are deeper. Use muffin cases with this tin. Mini muffin tins are mini versions of the muffin tin. Use mini muffin or petit four cases in this tin. To make square cupcakes use a special tin (see page 120).

cupcake tin

cases

measuring spoons

boxes

piping bag　　　　　**nozzles**

A word about ovens

All the recipes were tested on a convection oven. If you don't have a convection oven you may like to increase the temperature by 25 degrees – say from 350°F (180°C/Gas 4) to 375°F (190°C/Gas 5). Thankfully, cupcakes are quite tolerant and a few degrees difference in temperature will not hurt. Instead, keep an eye on the time; usually I give a cooking time from and to, so set the timer for the minimum time and check. If you don't have a timer on your oven it's worth going out and buying a cook's timer as some cupcakes cook in just five minutes – its easy to get distracted and let them burn. Once you have made a batch or two you will get to know your oven.

Food processor/table-top mixer/hand-held electric mixer

These are essential pieces of equipment for large batches of cupcakes and some frostings.

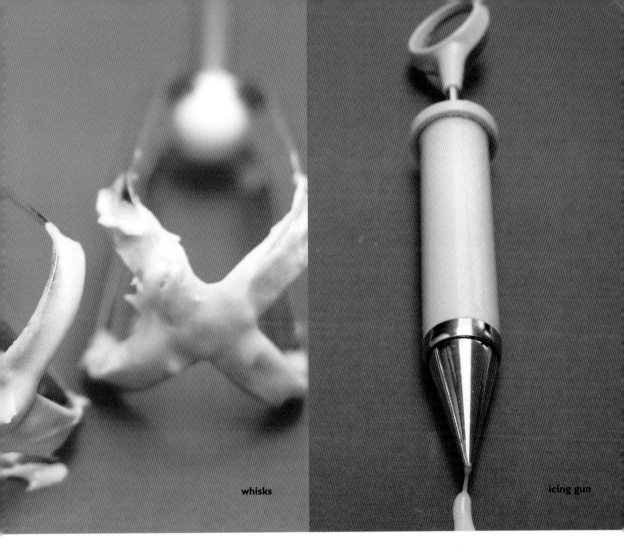

whisks

icing gun

Balloon whisk

A nice sturdy balloon whisk is best for whipping fresh cream. Electric appliances are faster and easier on the arm muscles but do encourage overwhipping.

Piping bags and nozzles

If you are going to indulge creative fantasies it's a good idea to have a selection of piping bags and nozzles. Buy ready-made plastic or fabric bags or make your own (see below).

Small homemade piping bags are useful for piping writing, small details and squiggles and they are easy to make. A large star nozzle is essential for piling generous swirls of buttercream on top of your cupcakes.

To make a paper piping bag

- Cut a 10-inch (25 cm) square of greaseproof paper or non-stick baking (parchment) paper.
- Fold the paper diagonally in half and roll into a cone.
- Fold the protruding points down and into the cone to secure the shape.
- Snip off the pointy end of the cone and use it as it is or drop a nozzle into the bag before piping.
- Half-fill with icing, then roll and fold the top edge down to close the bag.

Ingredients

Flour

In the recipes flour is always white unless specified otherwise. Self-raising flour is quick and easy to use and guarantees results as it includes a raising agent. If you can't find self-raising flour, you can make your own by sifting 1½ tsp baking powder and a pinch of salt with every cup of flour.

If using all-purpose flour a raising agent is usually added to the mix or the eggs should be whisked thoroughly to incorporate lots of air. Sifting also aerates the flour.

If measuring flour by volume (in cups) sift after measuring.

Whole wheat flour can be used but it tends to make a denser, heavier cake. I like it with chocolate. Make sure you buy wholewheat flour not strong whole wheat flour, which is used for bread-making.

Butter, fats and oils

You cannot beat the taste of butter in a cake mixture. I like to use a slightly salted butter for the cake mixture and unsalted butter for buttercream, if given the choice, but use whatever you have in the refrigerator. Cakes are so much easier to mix if the butter is at room temperature. If you forget to remove it from the refrigerator simply microwave for a few seconds to soften.

Soft tub margarine can just about be substituted for butter in a cake mixture, but it will not make a good tasting buttercream. Light, bland-tasting vegetable oils such as corn and sunflower oil can be used, particularly in American batter-style cupcake mixes. Because the buttery flavour is missing they are best mixed with strong flavours such as chocolate, vanilla, lemon and orange.

Eggs

I prefer free-range organic eggs and generally use size medium or large. If you are using medium eggs, you may need to add a little extra milk to get the right soft dropping consistency. Eggs at room temperature give the best results so remove from the refrigerator about 30 minutes before mixing.

Sugar

Superfine (berry) sugar is best for cake-making as it has small grains that dissolve quickly. Golden superfine sugar is supposedly less refined but it makes the cakes a darker beige colour, which I don't like, so I prefer to stick to the full-on refined sugar. Granulated sugar does not work so well and can give uneven, speckled or crunchy results.

Vanilla sugar gives a lovely flavour and aroma to cakes and is so easy to make at home. Simply immerse a few vanilla pods (beans) in the sugar and leave for a day or two before using. The vanilla will infuse the sugar with a glorious flavour and aroma. You can use lavender flowers in the same way.

Dark brown sugars and muscovado sugar add a distinctive flavour and colour. They tend to get a bit lumpy when stored, so crush them with a wooden spoon before mixing to remove any lumps. Lumps of sugar are really hard to remove once mixed with other ingredients.

Icing sugar is the finest of all sugars. It is used for icings as it dissolves quickly and easily. Always sift before mixing because lumps are much harder to remove once they are mixed with liquid. Do not use icing sugar in cake mixtures as it makes cakes with poor volume.

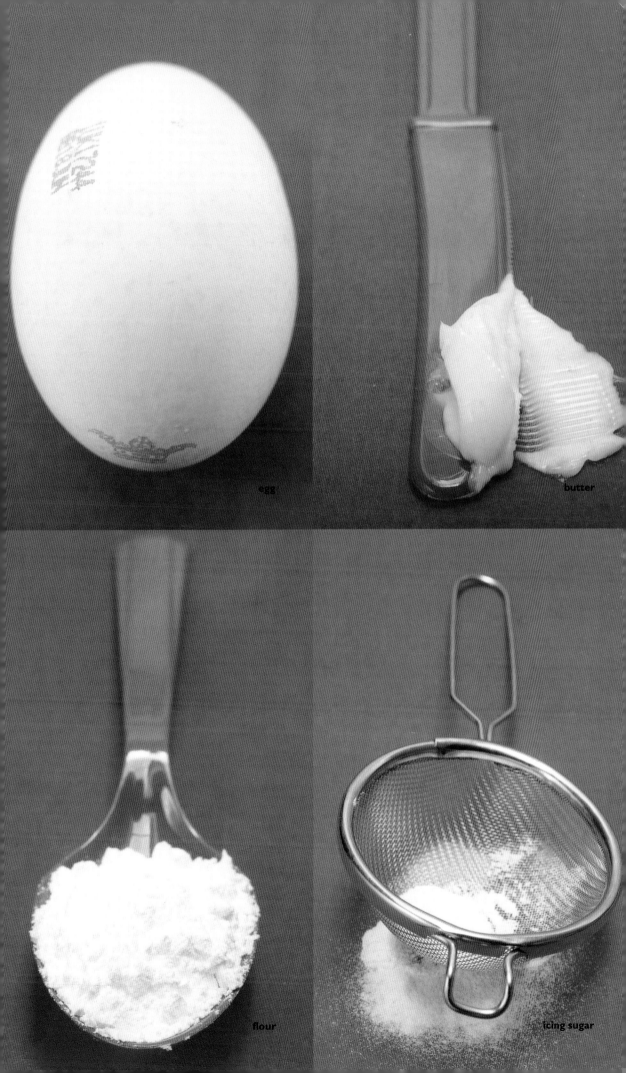

egg

butter

flour

icing sugar

Camp coffee

Camp coffee is one of those lovely nostalgic ingredients reminiscent of my mother's kitchen. It's a liquid mixture of coffee, chicory, sugar and water and it's what we always used to add coffee flavour to cakes and frostings before we became such a coffee drinking nation. The bottle is still fabulous to look at. I use it to give a lovely gentle coffee flavour. Really strong espresso coffee or instant coffee granules blended with a little liquid can also be used.

Frosted fruit, blossom and flowers

When making frosted flowers, make sure the flowers and petals are edible and have not been sprayed with pesticides. Lightly whisk an egg white in a small bowl, then, using a small brush, paint the fruit blossom or flowers sparingly with the egg white. Sprinkle with superfine (berry) sugar.

Sturdy fruits can be dipped into the sugar but it is better to sprinkle delicate petals. Allow to set and dry on non-stick baking (parchment) paper. These are best used on the day of making.

Spices

Spices lose their flavour over time, so buy in small quantities and use up quickly. Strength of smell is a good indicator of freshness. Taste as you go and add and adjust according to your palate – also a good excuse to eat raw cake mixture as it is one of the best cook's treats going.

Vanilla extract

Extract is preferable to essence because essence is a diluted version of extract and you will need to add more to get the same depth of flavour. The same applies to other extracts and essences such as peppermint, rose and almond.

Chocolate

Use a chocolate with a high cocoa solid content. Chocolate-flavoured cake covering does not taste like the real thing and is best avoided. White chocolate is tricky to melt as it burns extremely easily (see below). Step into any good chocolatier and you will be surrounded by inspiration. Chocolate flavoured with spices, chilli, rose, etc. can be substituted in the recipes.

Cocoa powder has a bitter chocolate flavour. It should not be confused with drinking chocolate, which is sweeter and milder. Sift cocoa powder before adding to cake mixtures. It is sometimes blended to a paste with a little water before mixing.

frosted flowers

chocolate curls

melted chocolate

Chocolate curls

To make chocolate curls, use a large bar of chocolate at room temperature. If it is too cold the chocolate will just crack instead of curling.

Using a sharp swivel potato peeler, shave off curls along the edge of the bar. To make fatter curls, use the flat side of the bar. If the chocolate will not curl, try running your finger along the bar first; the heat from your hand should soften it enough to make it work. This technique does need a bit of practice. If you don't have success, grate the chocolate instead or use crumbled flake bars.

Using a microwave to melt chocolate

• Break or chop the chocolate into small pieces so that it melts evenly and put in a clean, dry heatproof bowl.

• For small quantities use a low or medium setting and cook in short 30 second bursts. When you are more practiced, and for larger quantities, use a high setting. The time will vary enormously from brand to brand and depending on the initial temperature of the chocolate. Watch the chocolate very carefully as it scorches and burns easily and often looks like it hasn't melted when, in fact, it has. If you are melting chocolate with butter or liquids it will take less time.

chocolate leaf

bar of chocolate

Chocolate leaves

Well-defined, nicely shaped leaves are best.

- Make sure the leaves are washed and thoroughly dried.
- Using a small paintbrush, paint the underside of the leaves with melted chocolate. Avoid dripping the chocolate over the edge of the leaves or it will be difficult to peel them off when set. Leave to set.
- Apply a second coat and allow to set again.
- Carefully peel away the leaf from the chocolate, rather than the other way around.

Handle carefully – leaves break easily and will melt in the heat of your hand. Store in the refrigerator or freezer in a plastic container interleaved with non-stick baking (parchment) paper.

Melting chocolate over a pan of simmering water

This is the best method to use for white chocolate as it burns so easily.

- Break or chop the chocolate into small pieces so that it melts evenly and put it into a clean, dry, heatproof bowl.
- Choose a saucepan that the bowl will sit on without a gap around the sides. Makes enough water into the pan until it is one-third full and heat gently until simmering. Sit the bowl of chocolate on top, making sure that the base of the bowl does not touch the water.
- Stir the chocolate occasionally so that it heats evenly.
- Always cool before adding to cake mixtures as the heat can scramble the eggs.

Kitchen basics

What went wrong?

Things shouldn't go wrong, but sometimes it has to do with mood and the vibe in the kitchen and the music on the radio. Don't despair. Even if they are a little dry, or not as you really would like, it's hard to make a really 'ugly duckling' cupcake. Just smother with icing and decorate lavishly and no one will notice. For those of you who want answers, here are some suggestions:

Paper cases peel away from cake on cooling

Possible causes

- Cakes too dry or very moist.
- Cakes not removed from the mini-cake tin immediately. Remove cakes from the mini-cake tin as soon as they are out of the oven and cool on a wire rack to stop it happening next time.

Remedies

- Don't worry about it!
- Remove the cakes from the cases and cover with glacé icing; let it run down the sides of the cakes.

Your cakes were dry

Possible causes
- Ingredients weighed incorrectly.
- Cakes were overcooked.
- Cakes were not stored in an airtight container.

Remedy
- Lots of rich frosting.

Your cakes have heavy dense texture

Possible causes
- Too much liquid was added. Use measuring spoons next time.
- Not enough raising agent. Again best to use measuring spoons.
- Mixture curdled so it did not trap as much air. Add a little flour with the egg next time.

Remedy
- Fresh berries and whipped fresh cream.

Your cupcakes have peaked and cracked

Possible causes

- The oven was too hot.
- The cake mixture was too stiff; add more liquid next time or use a larger egg size.
- The paper cases were over-filled.

Remedies

- Level with a knife and decorate as usual.
- Level, dollop with buttercream and jam or lemon curd and replace the cut-off slice. Dust with icing sugar.

The cakes sank in the middle

Possible causes

- The mixture was too soft.
- There was too much baking powder or baking soda in the mixture.
- The oven was not up to temperature when the cakes were put in or did not reach the correct temperature. Check it with an oven thermometer.
- The oven was too hot when the cakes were put in so that they cooked too quickly on the outside. Check the oven temperature with an oven thermometer or reduce by 10 degrees.
- Cakes were not cooked when removed from the oven so they collapsed in the middle.

Remedy

- Disguise with glacé icing, melted chocolate or a fluffy frosting.

Hints and tips

Filling cupcake cases

For the prettiest and neatest results you want to fill the cases without spilling or splashing the mixture onto the sides and edges of the paper cases. If making a batter-style mixture it is easier to transfer the mixture to a jug, then simply makes it into the cases.

For a dropping consistency mixture it is best to fill the paper cases using two teaspoons. Simply scoop up a good teaspoonful of the mixture, then slide it off into the paper case using the second spoon. Don't overfill – the mixture will just leak out during cooking and make a mess.

To test when cupcakes are cooked

- Press the centre of the cake very lightly with your fingertip. It should spring back immediately without leaving an indentation. Do this quickly with the cakes half out of the oven because if they are not cooked you should get them back in as soon as possible or they will not rise fully.
- The kitchen will smell delicious.
- Listen for a sizzle. It will stop when they are ready.
- Look at the colour. Vanilla cupcakes should be a pale golden brown – don't let them become a dark golden brown or they will be overcooked and dry with a crisp top.

- For large cupcakes baked in a muffin case you could use a thin warm skewer. Insert it into the centre of one cake and remove it quickly. If there is wet cake mixture stuck to the skewer they are not ready.

Icing and decorating cakes

Obviously it is sensible to cool cakes completely before icing. Buttercream and whipped frostings do not like being put onto warm cakes and they will melt into unpleasant greasiness. However, it has to be said that slightly warm cakes covered in melted chocolate or glacé icing are food heaven.

Storing

Most cakes are best eaten on the day of making and should be stored in an airtight container. Cakes made with fresh fruit and fresh cream should be stored in a cool place or in the refrigerator on hot summer days and allowed to come to room temperature before eating.

If you want to freeze cupcakes then they are best frozen before being topped with icing. Put the cooked cakes on a baking tray, unwrapped, freeze them until they are hard and then transfer to freezer bags.

Decorations

sugar pearls and dragées

candy letters

sugar flakes

sanding sugar

sugar stars

Easy peasy cupcakes

Easy vanilla cupcakes

As I learnt to make these cupcakes with my mother we always did everything in imperial measures and, to be honest, I still find the best proportions are 4 oz flour, sugar and butter, and 2 eggs. After much trial and error, I think 112 g is the best equivalent, but in memory of my mum I am giving the imperial measures here, too. This basic all-in-one method is foolproof. Serve the cakes plain, warm from the oven adorned with a little icing sugar or topped with glacé icing (see page 148) of your choice. At the moment I am favouring glacé icing coloured turquoise to match my summer nail polish.

MAKES **18 REGULAR SIZE CAKES OR
12 MUFFIN SIZE CAKES**
PREPARATION TIME: **15 MINUTES**
COOKING TIME: **10-15 MINUTES**
PHOTOGRAPH: **PAGE 33**

½ cup (4 oz/112 g) very soft butter
½ cup (4 oz/112 g) superfine (berry) sugar
2 medium or large eggs
1 teaspoon vanilla extract, or to taste
¾ cup (4 oz/112 g) self-raising flour
1 level teaspoon baking powder
1 tablespoon milk, plus a little extra if necessary
TO DECORATE
icing sugar, for sprinkling (optional)
glacé icing (optional)
silver balls and hundreds and thousands, to decorate

Preheat the oven to 350°F (180°C/Gas 4) and put 18 regular paper cases into 2 x 12-hole cupcake tins or 12 muffin cases into a 12-hole muffin tin.

Put the butter in a sturdy mixing bowl – a bowl with a nice rounded bottom is easiest for mixing. I stand my bowl on a slightly damp folded tea towel to stop it moving about.

Beat the butter with a wooden spoon to make sure it is really soft. Add the superfine (berry) sugar, eggs, vanilla extract, flour, baking powder and milk and continue to beat vigorously until the mixture is well mixed and creamy. Take a scoop of the mixture, hold it above the bowl and tap it, allowing it to fall back into the bowl. If it is reluctant to budge add a little more milk to the mixture and try again.

This is called a dropping consistency. Using 2 teaspoons, divide the mixture among the paper cases and bake for 10–15 minutes until nicely risen and golden brown.

Remove the cakes from the tin and allow to cool on a wire rack. These cupcakes are delicious served slightly warm sprinkled with a little icing sugar. If using glacé icing, finish them off with a decoration of silver balls and hundreds and thousands.

VARIATION
Flavour the mixture with almond extract instead of vanilla, if you like.

FOOD PROCESSOR METHOD
Some would argue that using a food processor is easier, but I find it less satisfying and it does make more washing up. This method is best saved for large batches.

Simply put all the ingredients in the food processor and blend until smooth. Test for a dropping consistency, add a splash more milk if necessary and mix briefly again. Do not overmix or the cupcakes will not rise as beautifully.

SELF-RAISING FLOUR
Self-raising flour is quick and easy to use and has guaranteed results since it has a raising agent. If you can't find it, you can make your own by sifting 1 1/2 tsp of baking powder and a pinch of salt with every 1 cup of flour.

American-style cupcakes

A lot of American recipes include oil and sour cream in place of butter to make firmer textured cakes. Use an electric mixer or a hand-held electric mixer to introduce as much air as possible. Add 1 teaspoon vanilla extract to the cake mixture if you are using superfine rather than vanilla sugar.

MAKES **12 MUFFIN SIZE CAKES**
PREPARATION TIME: **35 MINUTES**
COOKING TIME: **15-20 MINUTES**
PHOTOGRAPH: **PAGE 34**

1 cup (7 oz/200 g) vanilla sugar (see page 14) or superfine (berry) sugar
2 eggs
4 heaping tablespoons thick sour cream
½ cup (4 fl oz/120 ml) sunflower or corn oil
1½ cups (7 oz/200 g) all-purpose flour
½ teaspoon baking powder
½ teaspoon baking soda
a large pinch of salt
FOR THE WHIPPED SOUR CREAM FROSTING
¼ cup (1¾ oz/50 g) soft butter
⅔ cup (3½ oz/110 g) icing sugar
4 heaping tablespoons thick sour cream
1 teaspoon vanilla extract, or to taste
fresh raspberries, grated chocolate, sprinkles or dragees of your choice, to decorate

Preheat the oven to 350°F (180°C/Gas 4) and put 12 paper muffin cases into a 12-hole muffin tin.

Put the sugar and eggs in a bowl and whisk with an electric hand-held whisk until thick and much paler in colour and the mixture leaves a trail when the whisk is lifted (you should be able to write your initials).

Whisk in the sour cream then gradually add the oil in a steady stream, whisking all the time. Sift together the flour, baking powder, baking soda and salt, then whisk this dry mixture into the egg mixture. Whisk until smooth and free from lumps.

Transfer the mixture to a jug and pour it into the muffin cases (they will be quite full).

Bake for 15–20 minutes until well risen and springy when pressed. Remove the cakes from the tin and allow to cool on a wire rack.

To make the frosting, put the butter and sugar in a bowl and whisk with an electric hand-held whisk until very pale. Add the sour cream and keep whisking to make a light frothy frosting. Add vanilla extract to taste. Swirl the frosting on top of the cakes and decorate as you wish.

Orange poppy seed cupcakes

MAKES **9 MUFFIN SIZE CAKES**
PREPARATION TIME: **35 MINUTES**
COOKING TIME: **10-15 MINUTES**
PHOTOGRAPH: **PAGE 37**

½ cup (4 oz/112 g) very soft butter
½ cup (4 oz/112 g) superfine (berry) sugar
2 eggs
finely grated zest of 1 large orange
2 tablespoons orange juice
¾ cup (4 oz/112 g) self-raising flour
1 level teaspoon baking powder
1 tablespoon poppy seeds, plus extra to decorate
FOR THE ORANGE GLACÉ ICING
½ cup (3½ oz/100 g) icing sugar
finely grated zest and juice of 2 oranges

Preheat the oven to 350°F (180°C/Gas 4) and put 9 paper muffin cases into a 12-hole muffin tin.

Put the butter in a bowl and beat to make sure it is really soft. Add the superfine (berry) sugar, eggs, orange zest and juice, flour and baking powder and beat vigorously until the mixture is well mixed and creamy. Take a scoop of the mixture, hold it above the bowl and tap it, allowing it to fall back into the bowl. If it is reluctant to budge add a little more juice to the mixture and try again. Fold in the poppy seeds.

Using 2 teaspoons, divide the mixture among the paper cases and bake for 10–15 minutes until nicely risen and golden brown. Remove from the tin and cool on a wire rack.

For the icing, sift the icing sugar into a bowl. Add the orange zest and juice and a splash of water and mix to make a thin icing. Spoon the icing onto the cakes, sprinkle with poppy seeds and allow to set.

Lemon cupcakes

Use unwaxed lemons and a good sharp grater to grate the lemon. As soon as you see the white pith appear stop grating – if the pith is included in the mixture it will make the cakes taste bitter.

MAKES **18 REGULAR SIZE CAKES**
PREPARATION TIME: **35 MINUTES**
COOKING TIME: **10-15 MINUTES**
PHOTOGRAPH: **PAGE 39**

½ cup (4 oz/112 g) very soft butter
½ cup (4 oz/112 g) superfine (berry) sugar
2 eggs
finely grated zest of 1 large lemon
1 tablespoon lemon juice, plus a little extra
if necessary
¾ cup (4 oz/112 g) self-raising flour
1 level teaspoon baking powder
FOR THE LEMON GLACÉ ICING
½ cup (3½ oz/100 g) icing sugar
finely grated zest and juice of 2 large lemons
yellow sugar flowers, to decorate

Preheat the oven to 350°F (180°C/Gas 4) and put 18 regular paper cases into 2 x 12-hole cupcake tins.

Put the butter in a bowl and beat until really soft. Add the superfine (berry) sugar, eggs, lemon zest and juice, flour and baking powder and beat vigorously until the mixture is creamy. Take a scoop of the mixture, hold it above the bowl and tap it, allowing it to fall back into the bowl. If it is reluctant to budge add a little more lemon juice to the mixture and try again.

Using 2 teaspoons, divide the mixture among the paper cases and bake for 10–15 minutes until nicely risen and golden brown. Remove the cakes from the tin and allow to cool on a wire rack until completely cold.

For the icing, sift the icing sugar into a bowl. Add the lemon zest and juice and a splash of water and mix to make a thin icing. Spoon onto the cupcakes, decorate with sugar flowers, then allow to set before serving.

Coconut cupcakes

These make a lovely summer breakfast served with a fruit smoothie.

MAKES **36 REGULAR SIZE CAKES**
PREPARATION TIME: **20 MINUTES**
COOKING TIME: **10-15 MINUTES**
PHOTOGRAPH: **PAGE 41**

½ cup (4½ oz/130 g) soft butter
1 cup (7 oz/200 g) superfine (berry) sugar
2 eggs, plus 2 egg whites
1 cup (4½ oz/130 g) self-raising flour
1 teaspoon baking powder
2 tablespoons milk
⅔ cup (2¾ oz/80 g) desiccated (dry unsweetened) coconut
TO DECORATE
1 quantity glacé icing (see page 148)
fresh coconut shavings
icing sugar, for sprinkling (optional)

Preheat the oven to 350°F (180°C/Gas 4) and put 36 regular paper cases into 3 × 12-hole cupcake tins.

Put the butter in a bowl and beat to make sure it is really soft. Add half the sugar, the whole eggs, flour, baking powder and milk.

Whisk the egg whites in a clean bowl until stiff, then fold in the remaining sugar and the desiccated (dry unsweetened) coconut. Fold into the cake mixture. Spoon the mixture into the cake cases and bake for 10–15 minutes until well risen.

Remove the cakes from the tins and allow to cool on a wire rack. Decorate with glacé icing and sprinkle coconut shavings on top. These cupcakes are also delicious served slightly warm sprinkled with a little icing sugar.

Spiced sultana cupcakes

MAKES **18 REGULAR SIZE CAKES**
PREPARATION TIME: **20 MINUTES**
COOKING TIME: **10-15 MINUTES**
PHOTOGRAPH: **PAGE 43**

½ cup (4 oz/112 g) very soft butter
½ cup (4 oz/112 g) golden superfine (berry) sugar
2 eggs
1 tablespoon milk, plus a little extra if necessary
¾ cup (4 oz/112 g) self-raising flour
1 level teaspoon baking powder
1 level teaspoon ground allspice
⅓ cup (2 oz/60 g) golden raisins
about 20 sugar cubes

Preheat the oven to 350°F (180°C/Gas 4). Put 18 paper cupcake cases into 2 × 12-hole cupcake tins.

Put the butter in a bowl and beat to make sure it is really soft. Add the sugar, eggs, milk, flour, baking powder and allspice and beat vigorously until the mixture is well mixed and creamy. Take a scoop of the mixture, hold it above the bowl and tap it, allowing it to fall back into the bowl. If it is reluctant to budge add a little more milk to the mixture and try again. Fold in the golden raisins.

Using 2 teaspoons, divide the mixture among the paper cases and bake for 10–15 minutes until nicely risen and golden brown. Roughly crush the sugar cubes and sprinkle on top. Remove from the tin and cool on a wire rack.

Light ginger cupcakes with cinnamon buttercream

These are also nice topped with glacé icing (see page 148) and coloured sprinkles (as shown in the picture on page 32).

MAKES **18 REGULAR SIZE CAKES**
PREPARATION TIME: **35 MINUTES**
COOKING TIME: **10-13 MINUTES**
PHOTOGRAPH: **PAGE 45**

½ cup (4 oz/112 g) very soft butter
⅔ cup (4 oz/112 g) dark brown soft sugar
2 eggs
1 tablespoon milk, plus a little extra if necessary
1 tablespoon molasses
1 cup (5 oz/150 g) self-raising flour
1 level teaspoon baking powder
1 heaping teaspoon ground ginger
6 pieces stem (preserved) ginger in syrup, drained and chopped

FOR THE CINNAMON BUTTERCREAM
¼ cup (1¼ oz/40 g) soft butter
1 teaspoon ground cinnamon
½ cup (2¾ oz/80 g) icing sugar
chopped or sliced stem ginger, to decorate

Preheat the oven to 350°F (180°C/Gas 4) and put 18 regular paper cupcake cases into 2 x 12-hole cupcake tins.

Put the butter in a bowl and beat to make sure it is really soft. Add the sugar (make sure it is lump free before you add it as sugar lumps are hard to beat out), eggs, milk, molasses, flour, baking powder and ginger and beat vigorously until the mixture is well mixed and creamy. Take a scoop of the mixture, hold it above the bowl and tap it, allowing it to fall back into the bowl. If it is reluctant to budge add a little more milk to the mixture and try again. Add the chopped ginger.

Using 2 teaspoons, divide the mixture among the paper cases and bake for 10–13 minutes until nicely risen and golden brown. Remove the cakes from the tins and allow to cool on a wire rack.

To make the buttercream, put the butter in a bowl and beat until it is really soft. Add the cinnamon and mix thoroughly. Add the icing sugar and beat to make a smooth creamy mixture. Add a little warm water to thin slightly. Swirl the buttercream on top of the cakes. Decorate with the chopped or sliced ginger and spoon a little of the syrup from the jar on top.

Coffee and walnut cupcakes

MAKES **11 MUFFIN SIZE CAKES**
PREPARATION TIME: **35 MINUTES**
COOKING TIME: **15-20 MINUTES**
PHOTOGRAPH: **PAGE 47**

1 cup (8 oz/250 g) superfine (berry) sugar
2 large eggs
1 tablespoon strong espresso or instant coffee granules
½ cup (3½ fl oz/100 ml) plain yogurt
½ cup (3½ fl oz/100 ml) sunflower oil
210g/7oz/1½ cups all-purpose flour
½ teaspoon baking powder
½ teaspoon baking soda
a large pinch of salt
¾ cup (2¾ oz/80 g) walnuts

FOR THE COFFEE FUDGE FROSTING
1–2 teaspoons instant coffee granules
2 tablespoons light cream (10%)
¾ cup (4 oz/126 g) light soft brown sugar
¼ cup (1¾ oz/50 g) soft butter
1¼ cups (7 oz/200 g) icing sugar
few walnut halves, roughly chopped

Preheat the oven to 350°F (180°C/Gas 4) and put 11 paper muffin cases into a 12-hole muffin tin.

Put the sugar and eggs in a large bowl and whisk with an electric hand-held whisk until thick and creamy and the mixture leaves a trail when the whisk is lifted (you should be able to write your initials).

Dissolve the coffee granules in 2 tablespoons of warm water. Mix with the yoghurt and oil, then whisk this mixture into the whisked egg mixture.

Sift together the flour, baking powder, baking soda and salt, then whisk this dry mixture into the egg mixture. Whisk until smooth and free from lumps.

Pour or spoon the mixture into the cake cases and bake for 15–17 minutes until well risen and springy to the touch. Remove the cakes from the tin and allow to cool on a wire rack.

To make the frosting, put the coffee granules, cream, sugar and butter in a small pan and heat gently until the sugar dissolves, stirring occasionally. When the sugar has completely dissolved, boil rapidly for 3 minutes.

Turn off the heat and sift in the icing sugar. Beat until smooth and thick enough to spread. Swirl on top of the cakes and sprinkle with the walnuts.

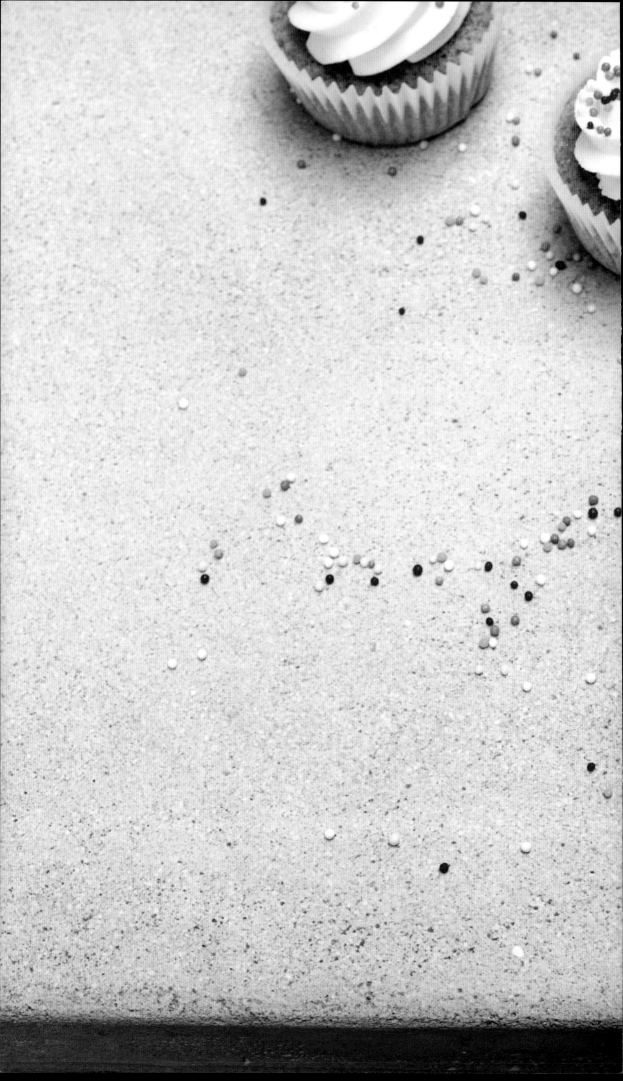

Carrot cupcakes with cream cheese icing

This recipe is for my lovely son Elliot who hasn't got a sweet tooth but loves carrot cake. He likes a very lemony topping, so I add the rind of two lemons, but for a more subtle flavour reduce by half.

MAKES **12 MUFFIN SIZE CAKES**
PREPARATION TIME: **45 MINUTES**
COOKING TIME: **15 MINUTES**
PHOTOGRAPH: **PAGE 48**

5½ oz (170 g) baby carrots
½ cup (4 oz/120 g) soft butter
¾ cup (4 oz/120 g) light soft brown sugar
2 large eggs
finely grated zest of 1 large orange
1 tablespoon lemon juice
1 teaspoon ground cinnamon
1 teaspoon ground allspice
a pinch of salt
¾ cup (3½ oz/100 g) self-raising flour
1 teaspoon baking powder
½ cup (1¾ oz/50 g) ground almonds
½ cup (1¾ oz/50 g) walnut or pecan halves, chopped
1 tablespoon milk
FOR THE CREAM CHEESE ICING
10 oz (300 g) cream cheese
⅓ cup (2 oz/60 g) icing sugar, sifted
finely grated zest of 2 lemons and the juice of 1 lemon
hundreds and thousands or coloured sprinkles, to decorate

Preheat the oven to 350°F (180°C/Gas 4) and put 12 paper muffin cases into a 12-hole muffin tin. Peel the carrots and grate finely. Wrap in a sheet of absorbent kitchen paper and squeeze over the sink to remove excess water.

Put the butter and sugar in a bowl and beat until really pale and creamy. Add the remaining ingredients and beat again. Add the grated carrot and mix thoroughly. Spoon the mixture into the paper cases and bake for 15 minutes until risen and springy to the touch. Remove from the tin and allow to cool on a wire rack.

To make the icing, put the cream cheese in a bowl and beat until smooth, then add the sugar and lemon zest and juice to taste. Chill the icing briefly to thicken if necessary, then swirl or pipe the icing on top of the cakes. Sprinkle with hundreds and thousands.

Almond cupcakes with jam and buttercream

These are for Deirdre, the photographer on the book. We have spent many pleasurable afternoons gossiping in my kitchen feasting on cakes and tea. The buttercream and jam combination is one of Deirdre's favourite things, so these are topped generously.

MAKES **11 LARGE OR MUFFIN SIZE CAKES**
PREPARATION TIME: **35 MINUTES**
COOKING TIME: **15-17 MINUTES**
PHOTOGRAPH: **PAGE 51**

⅔ cup (5 oz/150 g) very soft butter
⅔ cup (5 oz/150 g) superfine (berry) sugar
3 large or medium eggs
1 tablespoon milk (if using medium eggs)
¾ cup (3½ oz/100 g) self-raising flour
1 level teaspoon baking powder
½ cup (1¾ oz/50 g) ground almonds
few drops of almond extract
raspberry or strawberry jam, to serve
FOR THE BUTTERCREAM
⅓ cup (2¾ oz/80 g) very soft butter
1¼ cups (7 oz/200 g) icing sugar, plus extra for sprinkling
a drop of almond extract
1–2 tablespoons milk

Preheat the oven to 350°F (180°C/Gas 4) and put 11 large paper cupcake or muffin cases into a 12-hole muffin tin.

Put the butter in a bowl and beat to make sure it is really soft. Add the superfine (berry) sugar, eggs, milk (if using), flour, baking powder, ground almonds and almond extract and beat vigorously until the mixture is well mixed and creamy. Take a scoop of the mixture, hold it above the bowl and tap it, allowing it to fall back into the bowl. If it is reluctant to budge and if you used medium eggs add a little more milk and try again.

Using 2 teaspoons, divide the mixture among the paper cases and bake for 15–17 minutes until nicely risen and golden brown. Remove from the tin and allow to cool on a wire rack.

To make the buttercream, put the butter in a bowl and beat until it is really soft, then add the icing sugar, almond extract and milk and beat again to make a light creamy buttercream. Spoon or pipe the buttercream onto the cakes, top with a dollop of jam and sprinkle with icing sugar.

Chocolate cupcakes

Easy chocolate cupcakes

MAKES **12 REGULAR SIZE CAKES**
PREPARATION TIME: **45 MINUTES**
COOKING TIME: **10-15 MINUTES**
PHOTOGRAPH: **PAGE 55**

¼ cup (¾ oz/20 g) cocoa powder
½ cup (4 oz/112 g) very soft butter
½ cup (4 oz/112 g) superfine (berry) sugar
2 eggs
½ teaspoon vanilla extract, or to taste
1 tablespoon milk plus a little extra, if necessary
¾ cup (4 oz/112 g) self-raising flour
1 level teaspoon baking powder
FOR THE TOPPING
1 quantity of vanilla buttercream (see page 148),
coloured pink
icing sugar

Preheat the oven to 350°F (180°C/Gas 4) and put
12 regular paper cases into a 12-hole cupcake tin.

Put the cocoa powder and a little warm water in a
small bowl and blend to a paste.

Put the butter in a sturdy mixing bowl and beat with
a wooden spoon to make sure it is really soft. Add the
cocoa paste, superfine (berry) sugar, eggs, vanilla extract,
milk, the flour and baking powder and continue to beat
vigorously until the mixture is well mixed and creamy.
Take a scoop of the mixture, hold it above the bowl
and tap it, allowing it to fall back into the bowl. If it is
reluctant to budge add a little more milk to the mixture
and try again.

Using 2 teaspoons, divide the mixture among the paper
cases and bake for 10–15 minutes until nicely risen and
springy when pressed. Remove the cakes from the tin
and allow to cool on a wire rack.

When the cakes are cool, cut a thin slice from the
top of each and cut this in half. Top each cake with a
dollop of buttercream and stick the slices of cake into
the cream to resemble butterfly wings. Sprinkle with
icing sugar.

Peanut butter and chocolate cupcakes

Peanut butter sponge with a rich fudge icing was invented for my daughter Holly who is a peanut butter junkie. These are quite rich, so you may prefer to make 24 in regular size tins. If you do, then reduce the cooking time to 10 minutes.

MAKES **12 MUFFIN SIZE CAKES**
PREPARATION TIME: **45 MINUTES**
COOKING TIME: **22-25 MINUTES**
PHOTOGRAPH: **PAGE 57**

¾ cup (3½ oz/100 g) all-purpose flour
¾ cup (3½ oz/100 g) self-raising flour
¾ cup (6 oz/176 g) soft butter
¾ cup (6 oz/176 g) superfine (berry) sugar
3 eggs, lightly beaten
4 heaping tablespoons crunchy peanut butter
1 tablespoon milk, plus extra if necessary
FOR THE MILK CHOCOLATE FUDGE FROSTING
2½ oz (76 g) milk chocolate, broken into small pieces
¼ cup (1¾ oz/50 g) butter
¾ cup (4 oz/126 g) light brown sugar
¼ cup (2 fl oz/45 ml) heavy cream (35%)
1 cup (6 oz/175 g) icing sugar
2 teaspoons cocoa powder

Preheat the oven to 350°F (180°C/Gas 4) and put 12 muffin cases into a 12-hole muffin tin.

Sift the flours together. Put the butter and sugar in a large bowl and beat with an electric mixer or hand-held electric mixer until pale and fluffy. Gradually whisk in the egg a little at a time. Add the peanut butter and beat that in too. Scrape down the sides of the bowl and the whisks. Fold in the flours and add enough milk to make a soft dropping consistency.

Spoon the mixture into the paper cases and bake for 17–20 minutes until risen and springy to the touch. Remove the cakes from the tin and allow to cool on a wire rack.

To make the icing, put the chocolate, butter, sugar and cream in a heavy-based, preferably non-stick, saucepan and heat gently, stirring all the time until the sugar dissolves. Turn off the heat and sift in the icing sugar and cocoa powder. Beat thoroughly until smooth.

Swirl the icing on top of the cakes. Use a knife dipped in boiling water if the icing starts to set.

Chocolate pecan cupcakes with chocolate fudge icing

MAKES **10 MUFFIN SIZE CAKES**
PREPARATION TIME: **45 MINUTES**
COOKING TIME: **20-25 MINUTES**
PHOTOGRAPH: **PAGE 58**

¼ cup (¾ oz/26 g) cocoa powder
½ cup (4 oz/126 g) soft butter
¾ cup (4 oz/126 g) soft dark brown sugar
2 eggs
½ teaspoon vanilla extract, or to taste
1 tablespoon milk, plus a little extra if necessary
½ cup (2½ oz/76 g) whole wheat flour
1½ teaspoons baking powder
handful of pecans, roughly chopped
FOR THE CHOCOLATE FUDGE ICING
3½ oz (100 g) good-quality plain dark (semisweet) chocolate
3½ oz (100 g) milk chocolate
½ cup (4 oz/126 g) soft butter
¾ cup (3½ oz/100 g) icing sugar
sugar flowers, to decorate

Preheat the oven to 375°F (190°C/Gas 5) and put 10 muffin cases into a 12-hole muffin tin.

Put the cocoa powder and 3 tablespoons of warm water in a small bowl and blend to a paste.

Put the butter in a bowl and beat to make sure it is really soft. Add the cocoa paste, sugar, eggs, vanilla extract, milk, the flour and baking powder and mix thoroughly. Add the pecans.

Continue to beat vigorously until the mixture is well mixed and creamy. Take a scoop of the mixture, hold it above the bowl and tap it allowing, it to fall back into the bowl. If it is reluctant to budge add a little more milk to the mixture and try again.

Divide the mixture among the paper cases and bake for 10–15 minutes until nicely risen and springy when pressed. Remove the cakes from the tin and allow to cool on a wire rack.

To make the icing, put both chocolates in a heatproof bowl and melt in the microwave or over a pan of simmering water. Add the butter and icing sugar. Keep beating until thick and smooth. Allow to cool slightly until thick enough to spread, then swirl on top of the cakes.

Rich chocolate cakes with white chocolate ganache

If you want to keep the cakes in their cases, make half of the icing and swirl on top of the cakes. Don't worry about coating the sides.

MAKES **6 MUFFIN SIZE CAKES**
PREPARATION TIME: **45 MINUTES**
COOKING TIME: **20-25 MINUTES**
PHOTOGRAPH: **PAGE 61**

3½ oz (100 g) good-quality plain dark (semisweet) chocolate
¼ cup (2 oz/60 g) butter
⅓ cup (2 oz/60 g) soft light brown sugar
½ cup (1¾ oz/50 g) ground almonds
½ cup (¾ oz/25 g) fresh brown breadcrumbs
2 eggs, separated
FOR THE WHITE CHOCOLATE GANACHE
5 oz (150 g) good-quality white chocolate, chopped or chocolate chips
⅔ cup (5 fl oz/150 ml) heavy cream (35%)
crystallized (candied) flowers or petals or chocolate curls, to decorate

Preheat the oven to 350°F (180°C/Gas 4) and put 6 muffin cases in a 12-hole muffin tin.

Put the plain dark (semisweet) chocolate in a heatproof bowl and melt in the microwave or standing over a pan of simmering water. Remove from the heat and allow to cool slightly.

Put the butter and sugar in another bowl and beat until well mixed. Add the almonds, breadcrumbs and egg yolks and mix thoroughly. Add the slightly cooled chocolate.

Whisk the egg whites in a clean bowl until stiff, then lightly fold into the chocolate mixture. Spoon the mixture into the paper cases and bake for 15 minutes, or until risen and just springy and slightly peaking in the middle. Remove the cakes from the tin and allow to cool on a wire rack.

Remove the cakes from their cases and put back on the wire rack.

To make the icing, put the white chocolate in a heatproof bowl. Heat the cream in a pan until it just bubbles – watch carefully or it will boil over. Pour immediately onto the chocolate and allow to stand for 5 minutes, then whisk with a balloon whisk to make a smooth white chocolate ganache. Allow to cool until the mixture just coats the back of a spoon, whisking occasionally. Don't be tempted to put it into the refrigerator; it will set.

Pour the cooled ganache evenly over the cakes to cover the tops and sides. Decorate with crystallized (candied) flowers or chocolate curls, if you wish. Allow to set before serving.

Fortune-telling using tea leaves

I don't pretend to be an expert on this but it can add an extra dimension to an afternoon tea party. For those in the mood it has great opportunities for flirting and general theatrical behaviour.

Obviously tea bags are out here; we are talking proper good-quality tea made with proper tea leaves. Make the tea in the usual way, then pour it into a china cup – don't use a strainer or you will remove the leaves. A nice wide cup is best and makes reading easier.

Tell your victim to drink almost all the tea, leaving the tiniest bit in the bottom of the cup. To increase the drama tell them to concentrate hard on something that's been bothering them.

Get them to swirl the remaining tea three times in a clockwise direction, holding the cup in their left hand. Now up-end the cup onto a saucer and count to seven. Turn the cup the right way up, turning the handle of the cup to face the person reading the leaves.

The teacup handle represents the home and the present day. Things to the left represent events in the past and things to the right things in the future. Also patterns near the rim of the cup show things in the present time while those in the bottom show the future.

Now a lot of imagination and vision is required for the next bit as it may be really hard to identify any shapes in the leaves. Take your subject into account, concentrate hard (or look like you are doing so) and embellish what you see.

Some things to look out for

Rings are related to marriage.

Animal shapes: giraffe = trouble, cat = arguments, treachery or deception, cow = prosperity, goat = enemies are near.

Crown = success.

Star = good luck.

Marble chocolate and orange cupcakes

These are delicious served plain topped with a dusting of icing sugar or remove them from the cases and serve with hot chocolate sauce (see page 150) or chocolate orange glacé icing (see page 148) and sprinkles (as shown on page 65).

MAKES **12 MUFFIN SIZE CAKES**
PREPARATION TIME: **45 MINUTES**
COOKING TIME: **15-25 MINUTES**
PHOTOGRAPH: **PAGE 65**

2½ oz (76 g) good-quality plain dark (semisweet) chocolate, broken into pieces
¾ cup (6 oz/176 g) soft butter
¾ cup (6 oz/176 g) superfine (berry) sugar
3 eggs
1½ cups (7 oz/200 g) self-raising flour
1½ teaspoons baking powder
grated zest and juice of 1 orange
3 tablespoons milk

Preheat the oven to 375°F (190°C/Gas 5) and put 12 muffin cases into a 12-hole muffin tin.

Put the chocolate in a heatproof bowl and melt in the microwave or standing over a pan of simmering water.

Put the butter in a bowl and beat to make sure it is really soft. Add the sugar, eggs, flour and baking powder and beat thoroughly.

Put half the mixture in another bowl and fold in the melted chocolate. Add the orange rind and juice to the other half. Divide the milk between the 2 mixtures to make them the same consistency.

Put alternate spoonfuls of the mixtures into the paper cases and swirl a knife through each to make a marbled effect. Bake for 10–20 minutes until nicely risen and springy to the touch. Remove the cakes from the tin and allow to cool on a wire rack.

Chocolate snowballs

These cakes can be stored somewhere cool for up to three days, but not the refrigerator unless it is a really hot day.

MAKES **12–18 MUFFIN SIZE CAKES**
PREPARATION TIME: **45 MINUTES**
COOKING TIME: **15-20 MINUTES**
PHOTOGRAPH: **PAGES 66–67**

4 oz (125 g) block creamed coconut, roughly chopped
½ cup (1¾ oz/50 g) cocoa powder
3 cups (14 oz/400 g) self-raising flour
1 teaspoon baking powder
a large pinch of salt
1¼ cups (7 oz/225 g) light brown soft sugar
¾ cup (7 fl oz/200 ml) sunflower oil
FOR THE WHIPPED MALIBU CREAM
1¼ cups (10 fl oz/300 ml) heavy cream (35%)
1–2 tablespoons icing sugar
2–3 tablespoons Malibu or coconut liqueur
grated fresh or desiccated (dry unsweetened) coconut, to decorate

Preheat the oven to 350°F (180°C/Gas 4) and put 12–18 muffin cases in 2 x 12-hole muffin tins.

Put the chopped coconut into a bowl and pour over 2¾ cups (23 fl oz/650 ml) boiling water. Stir until dissolved, then allow to cool.

Put the dry ingredients in a bowl and mix thoroughly. Make a well in the centre, then add the oil and the dissolved coconut mixture. Beat thoroughly with a wooden spoon to make a smooth batter.

Divide the mixture among the paper cases and bake for 15–20 minutes until well risen and springy to the touch. Remove the cakes from the tin and allow to cool on a wire rack.

To make the icing, whip the cream until it just holds its shape, add the sugar and liqueur to taste and whip again. Spoon onto the cakes and sprinkle generously with coconut to decorate.

Chocolate and banana cupcakes

This makes a rich dark cupcake. Serious chocoholics should opt for the chocolate buttercream frosting (see page 148). For a less intense cupcake try the vanilla frosting, or vanilla buttercream (see page 148), which I like to divide into three portions and colour pretty pastel shades.

MAKES **24 REGULAR SIZE CAKES**
PREPARATION TIME: **45 MINUTES**
COOKING TIME: **10-13 MINUTES**
PHOTOGRAPH: **PAGES 69**

½ cup (4½ oz/130 g) soft butter
½ cup (4½ oz/130 g) superfine (berry) sugar
1 cup (4½ oz/130 g) self-raising flour
2 heaping tablespoons cocoa powder
3 eggs
3 ripe bananas
1 level teaspoon baking powder
FOR THE TOPPING
double quantity chocolate or vanilla buttercream (see page 148) or 1 quantity whipped sour cream frosting (see page 36)

Preheat the oven to 350°F (180°C/Gas 4) and put 24 regular paper cases into 2 x 12-hole cupcake tins.

Put the butter, sugar, flour, cocoa and eggs in a bowl and beat together until it is free from lumps.

Put the bananas in another bowl and mash, leaving a few chunks. Sprinkle the baking powder over the bananas and mix again. Tip the banana mixture into the chocolate mixture and stir together, keeping the banana chunks.

Divide the mixture among the paper cases and bake for 10–13 minutes until nicely risen and springy when pressed. Remove the cakes from the tins and allow to cool on a wire rack.

Swirl or pipe your chosen frosting on top of the cakes.

Teatime cupcakes

Light-as-a-feather cupcakes with rose cream

This recipe makes lots of cakes, but they don't keep very well, so freeze half for another day. The rose cream recipe is enough to ice half of the cakes.

MAKES **24 REGULAR SIZE CAKES**
PREPARATION TIME: **45 MINUTES**
COOKING TIME: **15-20 MINUTES**
PHOTOGRAPH: **PAGE 75**

⅓ cup (1¾ oz/50 g) self-raising flour
½ cup (1¾ oz/50 g) cornstarch
¼ cup (1¼ oz/40 g) butter
3 large eggs
½ cup (3½ oz/100 g) superfine (berry) sugar
FOR THE ROSE BUTTERCREAM
2 egg yolks
¾ cup (6 oz/175 g) butter
⅓ cup (2½ oz/75 g) superfine (berry) sugar
rose syrup, to taste
pink food colouring (optional)
crystallized (candied) rose petals, to decorate

Preheat the oven to 400°F (200°C/Gas 6) and put 24 regular paper cases into 2 x 12-hole cupcake tins.

Sift together the flour and the cornstarch 3 times. Put the butter in a pan and heat gently until melted. Allow to cool.

Put the eggs and sugar in a large, preferably glass, heatproof bowl. Stand the bowl over a pan of simmering water and whisk with an electric hand whisk until doubled in volume and pale. You should be able to write your initials with the trail from the whisk. If you have an electric tabletop mixer use that instead.

Sift half of the flour mixture into the egg mixture and fold in lightly using a large metal spoon or large plastic scraper.

Slowly drizzle half of the cooled melted butter into the mixture and fold in. Gradually fold in the remaining flour and butter. Divide the mixture among the paper cases and bake for 5–10 minutes until the cakes are risen and spring back when pressed with your fingertip. Remove the cakes from the tin and cool on a wire rack.

To make the rose cream, put the egg yolks in a bowl and whisk briefly. Put the butter in another bowl and beat with a wooden spoon until really soft.

Put the sugar and ¼ cup (2¼ fl oz/60 ml) water in a small heavy-based preferably non-stick pan and heat gently until the sugar has completely dissolved. Bring to the boil and boil rapidly until the temperature reaches 225°F (107°C) on a sugar thermometer.

Pour the sugar syrup onto the egg yolks, whisking all the time and keep whisking until the mixture is thick and cold. Add the very soft butter, rose syrup and food colouring (if using) and mix thoroughly until blended.

Spread the rose cream onto the cupcakes and decorate with crystallized (candied) rose petals.

Apple and blueberry cakes

MAKES **24 MUFFIN SIZE CAKES**
PREPARATION TIME: **45 MINUTES**
COOKING TIME: **15-20 MINUTES**
PHOTOGRAPH: **PAGE 76-77**

¾ cup (7 oz/200 g) soft butter
1¾ cups (8 oz/250 g) self-raising flour
1 cup (8 oz/250 g) superfine (berry) sugar
½ cup (1¾ oz/50 g) ground almonds
1 teaspoon baking powder
3 large eggs
few drops of vanilla extract
1 lb (450 g) cooking apples
3½ oz (100 g) blueberries
2 tablespoons milk
FOR THE CREAM CHEESE ICING
5 oz (150 g) cream cheese
1 teaspoon vanilla extract
squeeze of lemon juice
1–2 tablespoons icing sugar
frosted blueberries, to decorate

Preheat the oven to 350°F (180°C/Gas 4) and put
24 muffin cases in 2 x 12-hole muffin tins.

Put the butter in a bowl and beat to make sure it is
really soft. Add the flour, sugar, ground almonds, baking
powder, egg and vanilla extract and continue to beat
until well mixed.

Peel and finely chop the apple, then stir into the cake
mixture with the blueberries. Add enough milk to make
a soft dropping consistency.

Spoon the mixture into the muffin cases and bake for
15–20 minutes until well risen and springy to the touch.
Remove the cakes from the tin and allow to cool on a
wire rack.

To make the icing, put the cream cheese in a bowl and
beat until soft and fluffy. Add the vanilla extract and
lemon juice and icing sugar to taste. Beat again until well
mixed. Swirl or spread the icing on top of the cakes and
decorate with frosted blueberries.

Iced gems

These cakes definitely call for vintage cups and
saucers and ball gowns. Faded green, blue and pink
icing looks best.

MAKES **36 MINI MUFFIN SIZE CAKES**
PREPARATION TIME: **45 MINUTES**
COOKING TIME: **8-10 MINUTES**
PHOTOGRAPH: **PAGE 79**

1 cup (4 oz/126 g) self-raising flour
½ cup (4 oz/126 g) superfine (berry) sugar
1 teaspoon baking powder
½ cup (4 oz/126 g) soft butter
2 eggs
½ cup (1¾ oz/50 g) ground almonds
½ teaspoon almond extract, or to taste
3 tablespoons milk
FOR THE ICING
½ cup (4½ oz/130 g) butter
1½ cups (8 oz/260 g) icing sugar
2 teaspoons lemon juice
edible food colouring, sugar flowers and pretty cake
decorations of your choice, to decorate

Preheat the oven to 350°F (180°C/Gas 4) and put
36 mini muffin cases into 3 x 12-hole mini muffin tins.

To make the cakes, put all the ingredients into a bowl
and beat until well mixed. Divide the mixture among
the paper cases and bake for 8–10 minutes, or until
the cakes are well risen and springy to the touch.
Remove the cakes from the tins and allow to cool on
a wire rack.

To make the icing, put the butter in a bowl and beat
until really light and fluffy. Add the sugar and lemon
juice and beat to make a smooth icing that is stiff
enough to pipe.

Divide the icing among 4 small bowls and colour it
pretty pastel shades with food colouring. Spoon the
icing into a piping bag fitted with a star nozzle and pipe
rosettes onto the cake. Top each with a different sugar
flower, dragee or coloured ball.

Sticky ginger cupcakes

Serve plain or topped with glacé icing (see page 148) and edible flowers.

MAKES **24 REGULAR SIZE CAKES**
PREPARATION TIME: **35 MINUTES**
COOKING TIME: **8-10 MINUTES**
PHOTOGRAPH: **PAGES 80-81**

⅓ cup (3½ oz/110 g) molasses
⅓ cup (3½ oz/110 g) corn syrup
⅔ cup (3½ oz/110 g) dark muscovado or dark brown sugar
1¼ cups (9 fl oz/280 ml)
1⅔ cups (7½ oz/230 g) self-raising flour
1 teaspoon ground allspice
1 teaspoon ground cinnamon
1 teaspoon ground ginger
1 teaspoon baking soda
1 egg

Preheat the oven to 350°F (180°C/Gas 4) and put 24 regular muffin cases into 2 x 12-hole cupcake tins.

Put the molasses and corn syrup in a small pan and heat gently to mix.

Put the sugar and milk in another pan and heat gently until the sugar has dissolved. Cool.

Sift together the flour, spices and baking soda then add the milk mixture, syrup and molasses mixture and the egg and beat together until well mixed. Divide the mixture among the muffin cases and bake for 8–10 minutes until slightly risen and springy to the touch. Remove the cakes from the tins and allow to cool on a wire rack.

Iced cake selection

MAKES **18 REGULAR SIZE CAKES**
PREPARATION TIME: **45 MINUTES**
COOKING TIME: **10-15 MINUTES**
PHOTOGRAPH: **PAGE 83**

⅔ cup (5 oz/150 g) very soft butter
⅔ cup (5 oz/150 g) superfine (berry) sugar
3 eggs
1 cup (5 oz/150 g) self-raising flour
1½ level teaspoons baking powder
finely grated zest of ½ lemon
1 tablespoon milk
1 tablespoon cocoa powder
few drops of almond extract
FOR THE GLACÉ ICING
1¼ cups (7 oz/200 g) icing sugar
1 tablespoon cocoa powder, sifted
few drops of almond extract
finely grated zest of 1 lemon
rice paper flowers, crystallized rose petals, chocolate chips, to decorate

Preheat the oven to 180°C /350°F/Gas 4 and put 18 regular paper cases into 2 x 12-hole cupcake tins.

Put the butter in a bowl and beat to make sure it is really soft. Add the superfine (berry) sugar, eggs, flour and baking powder and beat until well mixed and creamy. Divide between 3 bowls. Add the lemon and a splash of milk to one bowl. Blend the cocoa and a little milk to a paste and mix it into another bowl, with a little milk if needed, and add the almond extract and a splash of milk to the remaining bowl.

Divide among the paper cases and bake for 10–15 minutes until nicely risen. Remove the cakes from the tins and cool on a wire rack.

For the icing, sift the icing sugar into a bowl. Add a splash of water to make a thick icing. Divide among 3 bowls. Add the cocoa powder and another splash of water to one bowl. Add the almond extract to another bowl, and finally add the lemon zest and a little lemon food colouring, if you fancy, to the last bowl. Spoon the icing onto the cakes, decorate as desired and allow to set.

Pear and blackcurrant crumble cupcakes

The crumble mixture can be replaced with crushed digestive biscuits and the fruit replaced with chopped apple and blackberries. Crumble mix freezes well. These are nice served warm with vanilla ice cream or lightly whipped double cream.

MAKES **24 REGULAR SIZE CAKES**
PREPARATION TIME: **45 MINUTES**
COOKING TIME: **16-21 MINUTES**
PHOTOGRAPH: **PAGE 87**

FOR THE CRUMBLE TOPPING
⅛ cup (1 oz/30 g) butter
½ cup (2 oz/60 g) all-purpose flour
¾ oz (20 g) superfine (berry) sugar
FOR THE CAKES
2 small ripe pears, peeled and chopped
handful of blackcurrants (frozen are fine)
2 tablespoons icing sugar, plus extra for dredging
½ cup (4 oz/125 g) very soft butter
½ cup (4 oz/125 g) vanilla sugar (see page 14)
or golden superfine (berry) sugar
2 eggs
1 cup (4 oz/125 g) self-raising flour
1 level teaspoon baking powder

Preheat the oven to 375°F (190°C/Gas 5) and put 24 regular paper cases into 2 × 12-hole cupcake tins.

To make the crumble, put the butter and flour into a bowl and, using your fingertips, rub the butter into the flour. Add the sugar and the tiniest splash of cold water to make a crumble consistency mixture.

Mix together the pears, blackcurrants and icing sugar and set aside.

Put the butter in a bowl and beat to make sure it is really soft. Add the sugar, eggs, flour and baking powder and continue to beat vigorously until the mixture is well mixed and creamy.

Divide the mixture among the paper cases and bake for 6 minutes. Remove from the oven, quickly spoon the fruit mixture on top and sprinkle with the crumble mixture. Bake for a further 10–15 minutes until tinged with brown. Remove the cakes from the tins and allow to cool on a wire rack. Serve warm dredged with icing sugar.

Orange blossom cakes

The antithesis of the American-style piled-high cupcake, these dainty springtime cakes are inspired by my fairy friend Ally. Decorate with sugared blossoms or flowers or something light and pretty. This recipe makes a lot, so freeze half of the mixture for another time.

MAKES **24–30 REGULAR SIZE CAKES**
PREPARATION TIME: **35 MINUTES**
COOKING TIME: **5-10 MINUTES**
PHOTOGRAPH: **PAGE 89**

3 large eggs
½ cup (3½ oz/100 g) superfine (berry) sugar
¾ cup (3½ oz/100 g) all-purpose flour
FOR THE ORANGE BLOSSOM ICING
2 cups (12 oz/350 g) icing sugar
juice of 1–2 medium oranges
orange blossom water, to taste
sugared blossoms or flowers (see page 16)
or something pretty, to decorate

Preheat the oven to 400°F (200°C/Gas 6) and put 24–30 regular paper cases in 2–3 x 12-hole cupcake tins.

Put the eggs and superfine (berry) sugar in a large, preferably glass, heatproof bowl. Stand the bowl over a pan of simmering water and with an electric hand whisk, whisk until pale, creamy and very thick. You should be able to write your initials with the trail from the whisk.

Remove the bowl from the heat and whisk until cool. Sift half of the flour into the mixture and fold in lightly and quickly with a large spatula or metal spoon. Add the remaining flour in the same way.

Working quite quickly, divide the mixture among the paper cases and bake for 5–10 minutes, or until well risen, springy to the touch and a lovely pale biscuit colour. Remove the cakes from the tin and allow to cool on a wire rack.

To make the icing, sift the icing sugar into a bowl and add enough orange juice to make a very thick spreading consistency. Add orange blossom water to taste and a little more orange juice if necessary. Spoon the icing onto the cakes and decorate with sugared blossoms or a decoration of your choice.

VARIATION
Cook the mixture in mini muffin cases (it will make about 48) and serve at drinks parties. They are perfect bite size and because the cake mixture is light, they're really suited for this sort of occasion. The orange blossom flavouring in the icing adds a note of interest. Don't forget to decorate extravagantly; with cakes this small and cute it's fun to play with scale. In summer decorate with whole frosted flowers or whole strawberries. In winter try chocolate leaves (see page 19), and if the party is really smart or it is a Christmas event, gild the chocolate leaves with edible gold leaf.

Raspberry cupcakes

These cakes are best eaten on the day of making.

MAKES **18 REGULAR SIZE CAKES**
PREPARATION TIME: **35 MINUTES**
COOKING TIME: **10-15 MINUTES**
PHOTOGRAPH: **PAGE 91**

½ cup (4 oz/126 g) very soft butter
½ cup (4 oz/126 g) vanilla sugar (see page 14)
or golden superfine (berry) sugar
2 eggs
1 tablespoon milk
1 cup (4 oz/126 g) self-raising flour
1 level teaspoon baking powder
handful of fresh raspberries, plus extra, to decorate
FOR THE VANILLA BUTTERCREAM
¾ cup (7 oz/200 g) soft butter
2¼ cups (14 oz/400 g) icing sugar
1 tablespoon
1 teaspoon vanilla extract, or to taste
white chocolate curls, to decorate

Preheat the oven to 350°F (180°C/Gas 4) and put
18 regular paper cases into 2 x 12-hole cupcake tins.

Put the butter in a bowl and beat to make sure it
is really soft. Add the sugar, eggs, milk, the flour and
baking powder and continue to beat vigorously until
the mixture is well mixed and creamy. Fold in the
raspberries.

Divide the mixture among the paper cases and bake
for 10–15 minutes until nicely risen and golden brown.
Remove the cakes from the tin and allow to cool on a
wire rack.

To make the buttercream, put the butter in a bowl
and beat until really soft. Add the icing sugar and
enough milk to make a light fluffy buttercream. Add
vanilla extract to taste. Swirl or pipe onto the cooled
cakes and decorate with raspberries and white
chocolate curls.

THOMPSON-NICOLA REGIONAL DISTRICT LIBRARY SYSTEM

Lemon curd and mascarpone cupcakes

Home-made lemon curd is nicest, but let's be honest: sometimes there are just not enough hours in the day for perfection. So if you are not in domestic goddess mode, embellish a good store-bought curd with a little grated zest to give it some zing and spend the time saved getting a manicure.

MAKES **18 REGULAR SIZE CAKES**
PREPARATION TIME: **35 MINUTES**
COOKING TIME: **10-15 MINUTES**
PHOTOGRAPH: **PAGE 91**

½ cup (4 oz/112 g) very soft butter
½ cup (4 oz/112 g) superfine (berry) sugar
2 eggs
finely grated zest of 1 large lemon
1 tablespoon milk, plus a little extra if necessary
¾ cup (4 oz/112 g) self-raising flour
1 level teaspoon baking powder
mascarpone
1 quantity lemon curd (see page 150)
icing sugar, for sprinkling

Preheat the oven to 350°F (180°C/Gas 4) and put 18 regular paper cases into 2 x 12-hole cupcake tins.

Put the butter in a bowl and beat to make sure it is really soft. Add the sugar, eggs, lemon zest, milk, flour and baking powder and beat vigorously until the mixture is well mixed and creamy. Take a scoop of the mixture, hold it above the bowl and tap it allowing it to fall back into the bowl. If it is reluctant to budge add a little more milk to the mixture and try again.

Using 2 teaspoons, divide the mixture among the paper cases and bake for 10–15 minutes until risen and golden brown. Remove the cakes from the tin and cool on a wire rack.

To serve, remove a slice from the top of each cake and top with a dollop of mascarpone and a generous dollop of lemon curd. Put the slice of sponge on top and sprinkle with icing sugar.

Lavender cakes

Make the most of lavender in your garden and use it for baking. It is so pretty and has a lovely subtle flavour. Make sure the flowers are clean and free from pesticides and bugs.

MAKES **24 REGULAR SIZE CAKES**
PREPARATION TIME: **45 MINUTES**
COOKING TIME: **15 MINUTES**
PHOTOGRAPH: **PAGE 95**

½ cup (3½ oz/100 g) vanilla or lavender sugar
(see page 14)
1 large egg
2 tablespoons plain yogurt
4 tablespoons (60 ml) sunflower or corn oil
¾ cup (3½ oz/100 g) all-purpose flour
¼ teaspoon baking powder
¼ teaspoon baking soda
a pinch of salt
1 teaspoon fresh lavender flowers, plus extra to decorate
1 quantity glacé or fondant icing (see page 148)

Preheat the oven to 350°F (180°C/Gas 4) and put 24 regular paper cases into 2 x 12-hole cupcake tins.

Put the sugar and egg in a large bowl and whisk with an electric hand whisk until thick and much paler in colour and the mixture leaves a trail when the whisk is lifted (you should be able to write your initials).

Whisk in the yoghurt then gradually add the oil in a steady stream, whisking all the time. Sift together the flour, baking powder, baking soda and salt, then whisk this dry mixture into the egg mixture. Whisk until smooth and free from lumps. Sprinkle in the lavender flowers. Transfer the mixture to a jug.

Pour the mixture into the cake cases and bake for 15 minutes until well risen and springy when pressed. Remove the cakes from the tins and allow to cool on a wire rack.

When cold, cover with the glacé or fondant icing and sprinkle with more lavender flowers.

Kids' cupcakes

Breakfast cupcakes

This one's for my good friend Riley who asked for a cupcake to fill the breakfast slot when time is short. Our mutual and rather lovely friend Fiona happens to be a prominent nutritionist, and tells me that these are packed with good stuff like fiber, essential fatty acids and vitamin E, and at only 125 calories each are good for weight-watching parents too. Serve with some fresh fruit or a glass of juice and your kids will be lively until lunch.

MAKES **18 REGULAR SIZE CAKES**
PREPARATION TIME: **20 MINUTES**
COOKING TIME: **10 MINUTES**
PHOTOGRAPH: **PAGE 98 (LEFT)**

1 cup (4½ oz/130 g) stoneground whole wheat flour
½ cup (1¾ oz/50 g) rolled oats
1 tablespoon pumpkin seeds
1 tablespoon sesame seeds
1 tablespoon sunflower seeds
1¾ oz (50 g/½ packet) dried berry mix (contains cranberries, blueberries, cherries and strawberries)
½ cup (2¾ oz/80 g) dark soft brown sugar
½ cup (3½ oz/100 g) soft margarine or butter
1 tablespoon baking powder
3 tablespoons milk
2 large eggs
TO SERVE (OPTIONAL)
runny honey or maple syrup
sesame seeds, for sprinkling

Preheat the oven to 350°F (180°C/Gas 4) and put 18 regular paper cases into 2 x 12-hole cupcake tins.

Put all the ingredients in a bowl and beat until well mixed. Beat for a further 2 minutes, then spoon the mixture into the paper cases and bake for 10 minutes.

These are nicest served warm from the oven but only the most bonkers parents get up to make a batch of cupcakes for breakfast. So store in the freezer and use for breakfast emergencies as required. Serve unadorned or topped with runny honey or maple syrup and a sprinkling of sesame seeds.

Caramellos

This is one for the teenagers – vanilla cake swirled with caramel and chunks of chocolate, topped generously with cream and more caramel, and nuts, and chocolate and calories. Oh, to be a teenage stick insect... The sticky toffee sauce is available in jars from supermarkets and delis. This also works well with Nutella.

MAKES **12 MUFFIN SIZE CAKES**
PREPARATION TIME: **45 MINUTES**
COOKING TIME: **15-20 MINUTES**
PHOTOGRAPH: **PAGE 98 (CENTER LEFT)**

⅔ cup (5 oz/150 g) very soft butter
⅔ cup (5 oz/150 g) superfine (berry) sugar
2 eggs, beaten
1 teaspoon vanilla extract, or to taste
1 cup (4 oz/126 g) self-raising flour
½ cup (2½ oz/76 g) all-purpose flour
4 oz (126 g) milk chocolate, roughly chopped
splash of milk
2 heaping tablespoons sticky toffee sauce, plus extra to decorate
FOR THE ICING AND DECORATION
mascarpone or whipped cream
icing sugar, to taste
vanilla extract, to taste
toasted slivered almonds

Preheat the oven to 350°F (180°C/Gas 4) and put 12 muffin cases into a 12-hole muffin tin.

Put all the cake ingredients into a bowl and beat until well mixed. Using 2 teaspoons, put a teaspoonful of the cake mixture into each paper case. Add a dollop of toffee sauce, then top with more cake mixture. Swirl a knife through the mixtures to blend them slightly together. Bake for 15–20 minutes until nicely risen and golden brown. Remove the cakes from the tins and cool on a wire rack.

To make the topping, put the mascarpone or cream in a bowl and flavour with sugar and vanilla to taste.

Swirl the topping on top of the cakes, drizzle with more toffee sauce and finally scatter with toasted almonds.

Nostalgic cupcakes

These are like the cupcakes I used to make with my mum, except we always called them fairy cakes. Decorate them with your favourite sweets but multi-coloured sprinkles or hundreds and thousands as we called them, dolly mixtures or tooth-breaking tiny silver balls were my mum's choices. My daughter says it's important to get lots of sweets on top. Minimalism is not the point here. These cakes are best eaten when the icing is sticky..

MAKES **18 REGULAR SIZE CAKES**
PREPARATION TIME: **20 MINUTES**
COOKING TIME: **10-15 MINUTES**
PHOTOGRAPH: **PAGE 98 (CENTER RIGHT)**

½ cup (4½ oz/130 g) very soft butter
½ cup (4½ oz/130 g) superfine (berry) sugar
2 eggs
½ teaspoon vanilla extract, to taste
1 cup (4½ oz/130 g) self-raising flour
1 level teaspoon baking powder
1 tablespoon milk, plus a little extra
TO DECORATE
glacé icing (see page 148)
your favourite sprinkles or sweets, buy loads – half the fun is sorting through for favourite colors

Preheat the oven to 350°F (180°C/Gas 4) and put 18 regular paper cases in 2 × 12-hole cupcake tins.

Put the butter in a bowl and beat to make sure it is really soft. Add the superfine (berry) sugar, eggs, vanilla extract, flour, baking powder and milk and continue to beat vigorously until the mixture is well mixed and creamy. Add a little more milk if necessary to make a soft dropping consistency.

Using 2 teaspoons, divide the mixture among the paper cases and bake for 10–15 minutes until nicely risen and golden brown. Remove the cakes from the tin and cool on a wire rack.

Spoon a little icing on the top of each cake. Decorate with your chosen sweets.

VARIATION
To make butterfly cakes, cut a top off the slice of each cake and cut in half. Put a blob of vanilla buttercream (see page 148) on the top of each cake and replace the slices to make wings. Add a little jam if you wish and dust generously with icing sugar.

Blueberry bliss cupcakes

MAKES **18 MUFFIN SIZE CAKES**
PREPARATION TIME: **45 MINUTES**
COOKING TIME: **15-20 MINUTES**
PHOTOGRAPH: **PAGE 98 (RIGHT)**

1 cup (7 oz/200 g) vanilla sugar (see page 14) or superfine (berry) sugar
2 eggs
finely grated rind of 1 orange
4 heaping tablespoons thick sour cream
½ cup (4 fl oz/120 ml) sunflower or corn oil
1½ cups (7 oz/200 g) all-purpose flour
½ teaspoon baking powder
½ teaspoon baking soda
a large pinch of salt
3½ oz (100 g) blueberries
FOR THE FROSTING
½ cup (3½ oz/100 g) soft butter
1⅓ cups (7 oz/200 g) icing sugar
2 heaping tablespoons thick sour cream
1 teaspoon vanilla extract, or to taste
blue food colouring
coloured sugar, for sprinkling

Preheat the oven to 350°F (180°C/Gas 4) and put 18 paper muffin cases into a 12-hole muffin tin.

Put the sugar and eggs in a large bowl and whisk with an electric hand-held whisk until thick and much paler in colour, and the mixture leaves a trail when the whisk is lifted (you should be able to write your initials). Whisk in the orange rind and sour cream, then gradually add the oil in a steady stream whisking all the time.

Sift together the all-purpose flour, baking powder, baking soda and salt, then whisk this dry mixture into the egg mixture. Whisk until smooth. Transfer the mix to a jug and mix in the blueberries.

Pour the mixture into the muffin cases (they will be quite full) and bake for 15–20 minutes until well risen and springy when pressed. Remove the cakes from the tin and allow to cool on a wire rack.

To make the icing, put the butter and sugar in a mixing bowl and whisk with an electric whisk until very pale. Add the sour cream and keep whisking until well mixed. Add vanilla extract to taste. Colour blue with food colouring. Swirl or pipe the icing on top of the cakes and sprinkle with coloured sugar.

Cookies and cream

MAKES **12 MUFFIN SIZE CAKES**
PREPARATION TIME: **45 MINUTES**
COOKING TIME: **20-25 MINUTES**
PHOTOGRAPH: **PAGE 99 (LEFT)**

5 graham crackers
7 oz (200 g) milk chocolate, chopped
1 cup (7 oz/200 g) vanilla sugar (see page 14)
or superfine (berry) sugar
2 eggs
4 heaping tablespoons thick sour cream
½ cup (4 fl oz/120 ml) sunflower or corn oil
1½ cups (7 oz/200 g) all-purpose flour
2 teaspoons cocoa powder
½ teaspoon baking powder
½ teaspoon baking soda
a large pinch of salt
FOR THE TOPPING
1½ quantities vanilla or chocolate buttercream
(see page 148)
sprinkles or decoration of your choice

Preheat the oven to 350°F (180°C/Gas 4) and put
12 paper muffin cases into a 12-hole muffin tin.

Crush the crackers, not too fine – you want to be
left with some recognisable chunks to give a layer of
crunch and divide among the paper cases. Put the
chocolate in a heatproof bowl and melt in the
microwave or standing over a pan of simmering water.
Allow to cool slightly.

Put the sugar and eggs in a bowl and whisk with an
electric hand whisk until thick and much paler in colour
and the mixture leaves a trail when the whisk is lifted
(you should be able to write your initials). Whisk in the
cream then gradually add the oil in a steady stream
whisking all the time. Whisk in the chocolate.

Sift together the flour, cocoa, baking powder, baking
soda and salt, then whisk this dry mixture into the
egg mixture. Whisk until smooth and free from lumps.
Transfer the mixture to a jug.

Pour the mixture into the muffin cases and bake for
15–20 minutes until well risen and springy when
pressed. Remove the cakes from the tin and allow
to cool on a wire rack.

Pipe or swirl your chosen buttercream on top and
decorate as you wish.

Marble chocolate chip cupcakes

These are most enjoyable and deliciously messy to
eat when the chocolate topping is still soft.

MAKES **18 REGULAR SIZE CAKES**
PREPARATION TIME: **45 MINUTES**
COOKING TIME: **20-25 MINUTES**
PHOTOGRAPH: **PAGE 99 (RIGHT)**

½ cup (4½ oz/130 g) very soft butter
½ cup (4½ oz/130 g) superfine (berry) sugar
2 eggs
1 teaspoon vanilla extract, or to taste
1 cup (4½ oz/130 g) self-raising flour
1 level teaspoon baking powder
2 tablespoons milk, plus a little extra, if necessary
2 heaping tablespoons cocoa powder
2 heaping tablespoons chocolate chips
TO DECORATE
8 oz (250 g) milk chocolate, broken into small pieces
chocolate chips

Preheat the oven to 350°F (180°C/Gas 4) and put
18 regular paper cases into 2 x 12-hole cupcake tins.

Put the butter in a bowl and beat to make sure it is
really soft. Add the sugar, eggs, vanilla extract, flour,
baking powder and milk and continue to beat until well
mixed and creamy.

Transfer half of the mixture to another bowl and add
the cocoa powder and chocolate chips. Add enough
milk to each mixture to make a dropping consistency.

Using 2 teaspoons, put alternate half-spoonfuls of the
mixtures into the paper cases. Run a knife through to
give the marbled effect. Bake for 15–20 minutes until
nicely risen and golden brown. Remove the cakes from
the tin and allow to cool on a wire rack.

Melt the chocolate then spread on top of the cakes.
Decorate with chocolate chips. Allow to set slightly, but
try to eat while the chocolate topping is soft.

Holly dolly cakes

These are for my lovely daughter who prefers a mix of strawberries and chocolate chips to flavour her ultimate cupcake. We use a mix of milk and white chocolate chips, but have recently been converted to some white chocolate and strawberry chocolate chips — they are such a pretty pink — that we came across in one of our favourite coffee bars.

MAKES **8–12 MUFFIN SIZE CAKES**
PREPARATION TIME: **45 MINUTES**
COOKING TIME: **15-20 MINUTES**
PHOTOGRAPH: **PAGE 99 (CENTER)**

8 oz (250 g) fresh strawberries
2 tablespoons icing sugar
squeeze of lemon juice
⅔ cup (5 oz/150 g) very soft butter
⅔ cup (5 oz/150 g) superfine (berry) sugar
2 eggs, beaten
vanilla extract, to taste
1 cup (4 oz/126 g) self-raising flour
½ cup (2½ oz/76 g) all-purpose flour
splash of milk
2¾ oz (80 g) chocolate chips
FOR THE ICING AND DECORATION
½ cup (3½ oz/100 g) soft butter
1¼ cups (7 oz/200 g) icing sugar
8–12 pretty strawberries

Preheat the oven to 375°F (190°C/Gas 5) and put 8–12 muffin cases into a 12-hole muffin tin.

Purée the strawberries in a blender, then push through a sieve to remove the seeds — not essential but nicer. Mix with the sugar and lemon juice to taste.

Put the butter in a bowl and beat until very soft, then add the superfine (berry) sugar and continue beating until light and fluffy. Gradually add the eggs, a little at a time, beating well after each addition. Add the vanilla extract. Sift together the flours, then sift again into the creamed mixture and fold in with a metal spoon. Add a splash of milk for a soft dropping consistency, then add the chocolate chips.

Using 2 teaspoons, put a teaspoonful of the cake mixture into each paper case. Add a generous spoonful of strawberry purée, then top with more cake mixture. You will have some strawberry purée left, so save this for the icing. Swirl a knife through the mixtures to blend them slightly together.

Bake for 15–20 minutes until nicely risen and golden brown. Remove the cakes from the tin and allow to cool on a wire rack.

To make the strawberry buttercream, put the butter in a bowl and beat until really soft, then add the sugar and beat until well mixed. Add enough of the remaining strawberry purée (about 2 tablespoons) to make a light fluffy icing.

Pile the icing on top of the cakes and top with the strawberries. Drizzle with any remaining purée, if you like.

CAK
HANDLE WI
984

Celebration cupcakes

Devil's food cupcakes

These cakes are perfect for any occasion, but spectacular at night with all the lights turned out, topped with indoor sparklers.

MAKES **12 MUFFIN SIZE CAKES**
PREPARATION TIME: **35 MINUTES**
COOKING TIME: **30-35 MINUTES**
PHOTOGRAPH: **PAGE 104-105**

2½ oz (76 g) plain dark (semisweet) chocolate, broken into small pieces
¾ cup (7 fl oz/200 ml) milk
½ cup (2½ oz/76 g) light soft brown sugar
⅓ cup (2½ oz/76 g) soft butter
¾ cup (6 oz/176 g) superfine (berry) sugar
2 eggs
1 tablespoon cocoa powder
1¼ cups (6 oz/176 g) all-purpose flour
1 teaspoon baking soda
FOR THE AMERICAN FROSTING
1 egg white
1¼ cups (7 oz/226 g) icing sugar

Preheat the oven to 350°F (180°C/Gas 4) and put 12 muffin cases in a 12-hole muffin tin.

Put the chocolate, milk and the brown sugar in a small heavy-based, preferably non-stick pan and heat very gently until the chocolate has melted and the sugar has dissolved. Allow to cool.

Put the butter in a bowl and beat until really soft. Add the superfine (berry) sugar and continue to beat until light and fluffy. Gradually add the eggs, beating after each addition.

Sift in the cocoa powder, flour and baking soda and fold in using a large metal spoon.

Slowly add the chocolate mixture to the cake mixture, then beat thoroughly until well mixed. Divide the mixture among the paper cases and bake for 10–15 minutes until risen and springy when pressed. Remove the cakes from the tin and allow to cool on a wire rack.

To make the frosting, put the egg white in a clean bowl and whisk until really stiff.

Put the sugar and ¼ cup (2¼ fl oz/60 ml) water in a heavy-based, preferably non-stick pan and heat gently until the sugar has dissolved. Then, without stirring, bring to the boil and boil until the temperature reads 240°F (115–120°C) on a sugar thermometer. Remove from the heat, let the bubbles subside, then pour it onto the egg white in a thin stream, whisking at the same time. Keep whisking until the mixture stands in soft peaks.

Swirl the frosting generously onto the cakes – be fairly speedy as the icing sets quite quickly.

Christmas cupcakes

These are really rich chocolate and chestnut cakes topped with gooey marshmallow frosting. Decorate them with something Christmassy.

MAKES **12 MUFFIN SIZE CAKES**
PREPARATION TIME: **45 MINUTES**
COOKING TIME: **25 MINUTES**
PHOTOGRAPH: **PAGE 108**

4½ oz (130 g) plain dark (semisweet) chocolate, chopped
½ x 15 oz (439 g) can chestnut purée (unsweetened)
½ cup (4 oz/120 g) soft butter
¾ cup (4 oz/120 g) light brown soft sugar
1 teaspoon ground cinnamon
1 teaspoon allspice
1 tablespoon cocoa powder
3 large eggs, separated
a pinch of salt
decorations of your choice
FOR THE MARSHMALLOW FROSTING
2 large egg whites
¾ cup (4½ oz/130 g) icing sugar
1 teaspoon liquid glucose
1 teaspoon vanilla extract
4 oz (120 g) mini marshmallows

Preheat the oven to 350°F (180°C/Gas 4) and put 12 foil muffin cases into a 12-hole muffin tin.

Put the chocolate in a heatproof bowl and melt in the microwave or standing over a pan of simmering water.

Meanwhile, put the chestnut purée, butter, sugar, cinnamon, allspice, cocoa powder and egg yolks in a bowl and beat together with a hand-held electric mixer. Alternatively, use a table-top mixer. Add the slightly cooled melted chocolate and keep beating until the mixture is light and fluffy. Add ¼ cup (2 fl oz/50 ml) warm water and whisk until blended.

Put the egg whites and salt in a clean bowl and whisk until stiff, then fold into the cake mixture. Divide the mixture among the muffin cases and bake for 15–20 minutes until the cakes have risen and feel springy when pressed. They may crack on top but this doesn't matter as they will be covered with icing. Remove the cakes from the tin and allow to cool on a wire rack.

To make the frosting, put all the ingredients except the marshmallows in a heatproof bowl. Stand the bowl over a pan of simmering water and whisk for 4 minutes, or until the icing is fairly thick. Add the marshmallows and keep whisking. The marshmallows will melt and the icing should thicken some more. It will take about 7–8 minutes of whisking in total. Allow to cool slightly, then spoon onto the cakes. Decorate as desired, something sparkly is good, and allow to set.

Halloween cupcakes

Black and white is a major influence in homes at the moment and liquorice has become trendy restaurant flavouring. I thought it would be perfect to combine the two to make Halloween cupcakes. If you don't like liquorice, and I must confess here that my son is violently opposed to it, make chocolate cakes instead. If you haven't got time to make a piping bag, buy ready-made tubes of black piping icing or gel.

MAKES **24 REGULAR SIZE CAKES**
PREPARATION TIME: **35 MINUTES**
COOKING TIME: **20-25 MINUTES**
PHOTOGRAPH: **PAGE 111**

7 oz (200 g) soft liquorice, finely chopped
⅔ cup (5 fl oz/150 ml) milk
1 cup (7 oz/200 g) superfine (berry) sugar
2 eggs
½ cup (4 fl oz/120 ml) sunflower or corn oil
1½ cups (7 oz/200 g) all-purpose flour
½ teaspoon baking powder
½ teaspoon baking soda
black food colouring
TO DECORATE
double quantity glacé icing coloured black (see page 148)
double quantity white glacé icing (see page 148)

Preheat the oven to 350°F (180°C/Gas 4) and put 24 regular paper cases into 2 x 12-hole cupcake tins.

Put the liquorice and milk in a heavy-based, preferably non-stick pan and heat gently to dissolve the liquorice, stirring all the time until softened and most of the liquorice has dissolved. Allow to cool slightly, then tip into a food processor and blend for a couple of minutes. Add the sugar and mix again.

Add the remaining ingredients and colour the mixture black with food colouring.

Divide the mixture among the paper cases and bake for 15–20 minutes until well risen and springy when pressed. Remove the cakes from the tin and allow to cool on a wire rack.

Cover half the cupcakes with most of the white glacé icing and half with most of the black glacé icing. Put the remaining icings into 2 small piping bags, snip a small hole in the end of each and pipe concentric circles. Quickly draw the point of a skewer through the circles starting from the inner circle to make a spider's web. Allow to set.

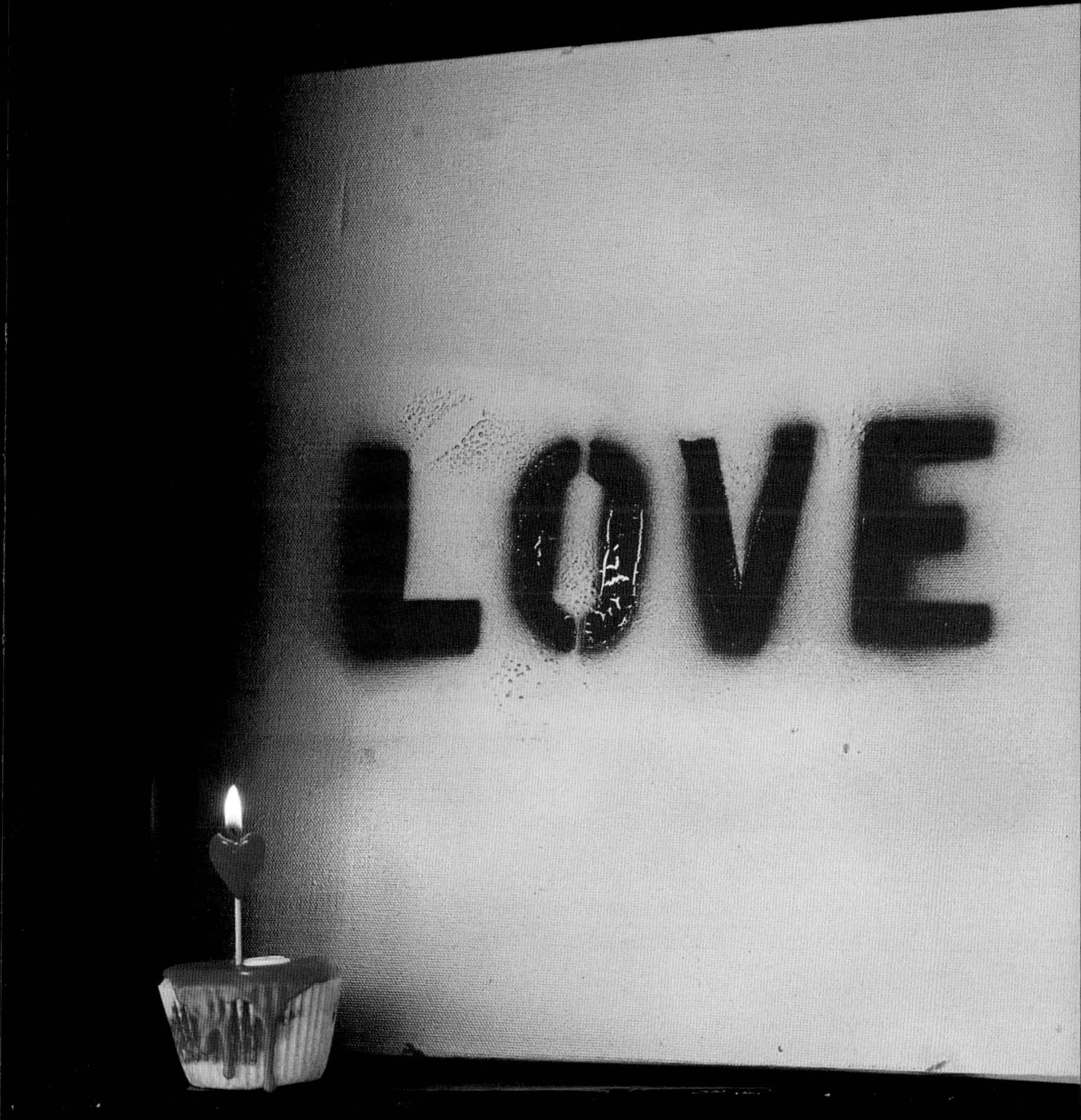
LOVE

Raspberry ripple Valentine cupcakes

The shops are full of heart-shaped sweets and chocolates around Valentine's Day so use them as decorations. Or stock up on tubes of love hearts and select your favourite message.

MAKES **8–12 MUFFIN SIZE CAKES**
PREPARATION TIME: **35 MINUTES**
COOKING TIME: **15-20 MINUTES**
PHOTOGRAPH: **PAGE 112-113**

7 oz (200 g) fresh raspberries
2 tablespoons icing sugar
squeeze of lemon juice
⅔ cup (5 oz/150 g) very soft unsalted butter
⅔ cup (5 oz/150 g) superfine (berry) sugar
2 eggs, beaten
1 teaspoon vanilla extract, or to taste
1 cup (4 oz/126 g) self-raising flour
½ cup (2½ oz/76 g) all-purpose flour
splash of milk
1 quantity glacé or fondant icing (see page 148), coloured pink or red, if you wish

Preheat the oven to 375°F (190°C/Gas 5) and put 8–12 muffin cases into a 12-hole muffin tin.

Push the raspberries through a sieve to remove the seeds, then mix with the icing sugar and lemon juice.

Put the butter in a bowl and beat to make sure it is really soft. Add the sugar and continue to beat until light and fluffy. Gradually add the eggs a little at a time, beating well after each addition. Add the vanilla extract.

Sift together the flours then sift again into the creamed mixture and fold in with a metal spoon. Add a splash of milk to give a soft dropping consistency.

Using 2 teaspoons, put a teaspoonful of the cake mixture into each paper case. Add a dollop of raspberry purée, then top with more cake mixture. Swirl a knife through the mixtures to blend them slightly together. Bake for 15–20 minutes until nicely risen and golden brown. Remove the cakes from the tin and cool on a wire rack.

Tint the icing pink or red or leave it white, if you prefer, and pipe or swirl on top of the cakes. Decorate as you wish.

White rose wedding cupcakes

These are little fruit cakes. Don't overfill the cases; you want enough room for a smooth layer of icing. If you like the look of these cakes but don't like fruit, follow one of the plain sponge recipes and decorate in the same way. White sugar roses are available from cake decorating shops. I like to top each with one huge rose, but you could use two or three smaller ones.

MAKES **18–24 MUFFIN SIZE CAKES**
PREPARATION TIME: **45 MINUTES + 8 HOURS SOAKING**
COOKING TIME: **20-25 MINUTES**
PHOTOGRAPH: **PAGE 115**

1¼ cups (7 oz/225 g) mixed dried fruit
1¾ oz (50 g) stoned (pitted) ready-to-eat prunes, chopped
1 tea bag
1¾ cups (8 oz/250 g) self-raising flour
2 teaspoons ground allspice
1 level teaspoon baking powder
¾ cup (4½ oz/130 g) dark soft brown sugar
½ cup (4½ oz/130 g) soft butter
2 tablespoons molasses
zest of 1 orange
2 eggs
TO DECORATE
double quantity at least fondant icing or glacé icing (see page 148)
white sugar roses

Preheat the oven to 150°C/300°F/Gas 2 and put 18–24 silver or gold foil muffin cases into 2 x 12-hole muffin tins.

Put the fruit and prunes in a heatproof bowl and mix together. Set aside.

Put the tea bag in another heatproof bowl and pour over 1¼ cups (10 fl oz/300 ml) boiling water. Allow to brew for a couple of minutes, then pour onto the fruit and allow to soak overnight.

Sift together the flour, allspice and baking powder. Put the sugar and butter in a bowl and beat until soft and fluffy. Add the fruit, molasses and orange zest and beat again. Add the flour mixture and the eggs and mix thoroughly.

Using 2 teaspoons, divide the mixture among the paper cases and spread with the back of a teaspoon to level the surface. They should be no more than two-thirds full. Bake for 20–25 minutes until the cakes feel firm when pressed gently. Remove the cakes from the tin and allow to cool on a wire rack.

Cover the tops of the cakes completely with the icing and decorate with sugar roses. Allow to set completely.

Easter cakes

The shops are full of inspiration around Eastertime. I adore Simnel cake, but it's hard to make that cupcake size, so make these fruity, almond cakes instead. If children are coming round for an egg hunt, make a batch of vanilla cupcakes as well and top generously with chocolate buttercream (see page 148) and chocolate eggs and sweets.

MAKES **12 MUFFIN SIZE CAKES OR
24 REGULAR SIZE CAKES**
PREPARATION TIME: **35 MINUTES**
COOKING TIME: **10-13 MINUTES**
PHOTOGRAPH: **PAGE 117**

½ cup (4½ oz/130 g) soft butter
½ cup (4½ oz/130 g) superfine (berry) sugar
1 cup (4½ oz/130 g) self-raising flour
1 level teaspoon baking powder
3 eggs
2 heaping tablespoons ground almonds
½ cup (1¾ oz/50 g) toasted slivered almonds, roughly chopped
2 large pinches of ground cinnamon and ground nutmeg
¼ cup (1¾ oz/50 g) chopped mixed peel
½ cup (3½ oz/100 g) golden raisins
finely grated rind of 1 lemon
FOR THE WHIPPED LEMON CREAM FROSTING
¼ cup (1¾ oz/50 g) soft butter
⅔ cup (3½ oz/110 g) icing sugar
4 heaping tablespoons thick sour cream
finely grated rind of 1 lemon
pale yellow food colouring (optional)
chocolate-covered mini eggs, sugar flowers or sprinkles, to decorate

Preheat the oven to 350°F (180°C/Gas 4) and put 12 muffin cases into a 12-hole muffin tin or put 24 regular cases into 2 x 12-hole cupcake tins.

Put the butter, sugar, flour, baking powder and eggs in a bowl and beat together until free from lumps. Add the almonds, cinnamon, ground nutmeg, mixed peel, golden raisins and lemon rind and beat thoroughly until mixed.

Divide the mixture among the paper cases and cook for 10–13 minutes until nicely risen and springy when pressed. Remove the cakes from the tins and allow to cool on a wire rack.

To make the frosting, put the butter and sugar in a sturdy mixing bowl and whisk together with a hand-held electric mixer until very pale. Add the sour cream and lemon rind and keep whisking to make a light frothy icing. Colour the frosting pale yellow with the food colouring, if using, then swirl on top of the cakes and decorate as you wish.

Disco cakes

These are dark chocolate mud cakes topped with sparkly icing. They can be adapted as you wish – great for weddings, birthday parties, thank-you gifts. If you want to write a message on the cakes use edible piping gel pens, which are widely available from supermarkets, before sprinkling with the glitter. Edible glitter/sparkle powder is also available from cake-decorating suppliers.

MAKES **12–16 MUFFIN SIZE CAKES OR
24 REGULAR SIZE CAKES**
PREPARATION TIME: **45 MINUTES**
COOKING TIME: **15-20 MINUTES**
PHOTOGRAPH: **PAGE 119**

½ cup (3½ oz/100 g) superfine (berry) sugar
½ cup (3½ oz/100 g) soft dark muscovado or dark brown sugar
2 eggs
4 heaping tablespoons thick sour cream
½ cup (4 fl oz/120 ml) sunflower or corn oil
1 cup (5 oz/150 g) all-purpose flour
½ cup (1¾ oz/50 g) cocoa powder
½ teaspoon baking powder
½ teaspoon baking soda
a large pinch of salt
1¾ oz (50 g) good-quality plain dark (semisweet) chocolate, melted
FOR THE ICING AND DECORATION
double quantity of glacé icing (see page 148) coloured as desired
edible glitter/sparkle powder

Preheat the oven to 350°F (180°C/Gas 4) and put 12–16 paper muffin cases into 2 x 12-hole muffin tins or 24 regular cases into 2 x 12-hole cupcake tins.

Put the sugars and eggs in a bowl and whisk with an electric hand-held whisk until thick and much paler in colour and the mixture leaves a trail when the whisk is lifted (you should be able to write your initials). Whisk in the sour cream, then gradually add the oil in a steady stream, whisking all the time.

Sift together the flour, cocoa powder, baking powder, baking soda and salt, then whisk this dry mixture into the egg mixture. Whisk until smooth and free from lumps. Finally, whisk in the melted chocolate. Add 2 tablespoons of water if the mixture is too thick.

Transfer the mixture to a jug and pour into the muffin cases so that they are half full. Bake for 15–20 minutes until well risen and springy when pressed. Remove the cakes from the tins and allow them to cool completely on a wire rack.

Cover the cakes with glacé icing and sprinkle with disco sparkle.

Fondant iced cakes

These cakes are baked in my favourite latest discovery – a mini square cake pan set! It's a large square pan that is divided into 16 little square tins and it's fabulous for making mini celebration cakes. You will also need to buy mini square cake pan liners – cute little cross-shaped pieces of greaseproof that fit the pans exactly.

This is a basic recipe that can be adapted and flavoured to suit the occasion – Mother's Day, wedding, birthday, good luck, well done, sorry, tough luck…

MAKES **16 MINI SQUARE CAKES**
PREPARATION TIME: **45 MINUTES**
COOKING TIME: **15-17 MINUTES**
PHOTOGRAPH: **PAGE 121**

1 cup (8 oz/250 g) very soft butter
1 cup (8 oz/250 g) superfine (berry) sugar
4 large eggs
vanilla extract, to taste or grated rind of 3 lemons and a few drops of lemon extract
1¾ cups (8 oz/250 g) self-raising flour
splash of milk (optional)
FOR THE FILLING AND DECORATION
apricot or raspberry jam
vanilla buttercream (see page 148)
ready-made rolling fondant icing, coloured as desired (optional)
coloured glacé icing (see page 148)
glitter powder

Preheat the oven to 350°F (180°C/Gas 4) and put 16 pan liners into the cake tins.

Put the butter in a bowl and beat to make sure it is really soft. Add the sugar and continue to beat until light and fluffy – as this is a fairly large quantity you might like to use a hand whisk or table-top mixer. Gradually add the eggs a little at a time, beating well after each addition. Add the vanilla extract or lemon rind and extract.

Sift the flour, then sift again into the creamed mixture and fold in with a metal spoon. Add a splash of milk if necessary to give a soft dropping consistency.

Carefully divide the mixture among the lined tins, trying to fill them evenly. Bake for about 15–17 minutes until risen to the top of the tins and slightly browned (they will not go very brown). Allow to cool in the tins on a wire rack.

Remove the cakes from the cases if you wish, split in

Once cooked the cakes can be removed from their cases, split and filled with jam and buttercream and then topped with rolled-out fondant icing. They do look adorable in their little paper cases so I sometimes leave them plain in their cases and just ice the top with fondant or glacé icing (see page 148). So, get a good selection of edible colouring and piping bags and let your imagination run wild.

half and sandwich together with jam and buttercream. Brush the top of each cake with a little more jam.

Roll out the fondant icing between two sheets of non-stick baking (parchment) paper until thin. Cut out cross-shaped pieces of fondant using a clean pan liner as a guide. Use to cover the top of each cake. Decorate with icing messages, flowers, etc. using coloured glacé icing and glitter powder.

Dessert cupcakes

Bitter chocolate and peppermint cupcakes

MAKES **12–16 MUFFIN SIZE CAKES**
PREPARATION TIME: **45 MINUTES**
COOKING TIME: **15-25 MINUTES**
PHOTOGRAPH: **PAGE 125**

5 oz (150 g) good-quality plain dark (semisweet)
chocolate, broken into pieces
¾ cup (6 oz/176 g) soft butter
¾ cup (6 oz/176 g) superfine (berry) sugar
3 eggs
1½ cups (7 oz/200 g) self-raising flour
1 tablespoon cocoa powder
1½ teaspoons baking powder
1 tablespoon milk, plus a little extra, if necessary
FOR THE PEPPERMINT CREAM
1¼ cups (10 fl oz/300 ml) heavy cream (35%)
green food colouring
1 tablespoon icing sugar
½ teaspoon peppermint extract
FOR THE PEPPERMINT ICING
1 cup (7 oz/200 g) icing sugar
1 teaspoon peppermint extract
green food colouring

Preheat the oven to 350°F (180°C/Gas 4) and
put 12–16 paper muffin cases into 1–2 x 12-hole
muffin tins.

Put the chocolate into a heatproof bowl and melt in the
microwave or standing over a pan of simmering water.

Put the butter in a bowl and beat to make sure it is
really soft. Add the superfine (berry) sugar, eggs, flour,
cocoa, baking powder and 1 tablespoon of milk and
beat thoroughly until well mixed. Add more milk if
necessary, to make a soft dropping consistency.

Divide the mixture among the paper cases and bake
for 10–20 minutes until nicely risen and springy to the
touch. Remove the cakes from the tin and allow to cool
on a wire rack.

To make the peppermint cream, put the cream in a bowl
and colour it pale green with food colouring. Whip until
it stands in soft peaks. Add the sugar and peppermint
extract and whip again until blended. Remove the cakes
from their cases, split in half horizontally and sandwich
them together with the cream.

To make the peppermint icing, sift the icing sugar into a
bowl and mix with enough water to make a runny icing.
Add peppermint extract to taste. Colour green with
food colouring. Spoon the icing onto the cakes, letting it
fall down the sides. Allow to set before serving.

Sticky toffee and date muffins

MAKES **12 MUFFIN SIZE CAKES**
PREPARATION TIME: **45 MINUTES**
COOKING TIME: **20 MINUTES**
PHOTOGRAPH: **PAGE 129 (TOP)**

8 oz (250 g) stoned (pitted) dates, roughly chopped
¼ cup (1¾ oz/50 g) butter
⅔ cups (7 oz/225 g) self-raising flour
1 teaspoon baking soda
2 teaspoons baking powder
2 teaspoons ground allspice
1 teaspoons ground cinnamon
1 cup (6 oz/175 g) light muscovado or dark brown sugar
2 large eggs
decoration of your choice, to serve
FOR THE TOFFEE SAUCE
¼ cup (1¾ oz/50 g) butter
½ cup (2½ oz/75 g) light muscovado or dark brown sugar
½ cup (3½ fl oz/100 ml) heavy cream (35%)

Preheat the oven to 350°F (180°C/Gas 4) and put 12 muffin cases into a 12-hole muffin tin.

Put the dates and butter in a heatproof bowl and pour over 250 ml/8 fl oz/1 cup boiling water. Allow to stand for a few minutes to cool a little, then blend to a smooth purée in a food processor.

Sift together the flour, baking soda, baking powder and spices, then add the sugar, eggs and date purée and stir until just combined. Spoon the mixture into the muffin cases and bake for 15 minutes until well risen and springy when pressed. Remove the cakes from the tin and allow to cool on a wire rack.

To make the sauce, put the butter, sugar and half of the cream into a pan and heat gently, stirring until melted. Alternatively, put everything in a glass heatproof bowl and microwave on high for 2 minutes, then stir and cook for a further 2 minutes until the sauce is melted and smooth.

Serve the cakes with the warm toffee sauce and top with a decoration of your choice.

Moist apple cakes

MAKES **16 MUFFIN SIZE CAKES**
PREPARATION TIME: **45 MINUTES**
COOKING TIME: **15-20 MINUTES**
PHOTOGRAPH: **PAGE 129 (BOTTOM)**

14 oz (400 g) eating apples
zest and juice of 1 lemon
½ cup (4 oz/126 g) soft butter
1 cup (6 oz/176 g) dark soft brown sugar
1 teaspoon ground cinnamon
1 teaspoon ground allspice
2 eggs
⅓ cup (1¾ oz/50 g) whole wheat flour
1¼ cups (5½ oz/160 g) self-raising flour
1 teaspoon baking powder
1 tablespoon milk, plus a little extra, if necessary
coloured sugar, to decorate
FOR THE CRUSHED BERRY CREAM
1¼ cups (10 fl oz/300 ml) heavy cream (35%)
1 tablespoon icing sugar
2 tablespoons blackberries

Preheat the oven to 350°F (180°C/Gas 4) and put 16 muffin cases in 2 x 12-hole muffin tins.

Peel, core and finely chop the apples. Toss the apples with the lemon zest and juice. Set aside.

Put the butter and sugar in a bowl and beat until light and soft. Add the spices and beat again. Add the eggs a little at a time, beating well as you go. Add the flours, baking powder and chopped apples and mix thoroughly. Add enough milk to make a soft dropping consistency.

Spoon the mixture into the muffin cases and bake for 15–20 minutes until they are well risen and firm to the touch. Remove the cakes from the tin and allow to cool on a wire rack.

To make the crushed berry cream whip the cream with the sugar until it just holds its shape. Fold in the berries, crushing them slightly to release the juice. Pile onto the cakes and top with coloured sugar.

Banoffee cupcakes

These cupcakes are a heavenly mixture of sponge, caramel, banana and cream.

MAKES **9 MUFFIN SIZE CAKES**
PREPARATION TIME: **45 MINUTES**
COOKING TIME: **35 MINUTES**
PHOTOGRAPH: **PAGE 131**

¼ cup (1¾ oz/50 g) very soft butter
¼ cup (1¾ oz/50 g) superfine (berry) sugar
1 egg
2 tablespoons milk
⅓ cup (1¾ oz/50 g) self-raising flour
⅓ cup (2 oz/60 g) finely chopped hazelnuts, pecans or walnuts
1 level teaspoon baking powder
FOR THE CARAMEL FILLING
½ cup (3½ oz/100 g) butter
½ cup (3½ oz/100 g) soft brown sugar
14 oz (397 g) can condensed milk
FOR THE TOPPING
2 bananas
crème fraîche or whipped cream
grated chocolate or chocolate curls

Preheat the oven to 375°F (190°C/Gas 5) and put 9 sturdy paper muffin cases into a 12-hole muffin tin.

Put the butter in a bowl and beat to make sure it is really soft. Add the superfine (berry) sugar, egg, milk, the flour, nuts and baking powder and continue to beat vigorously until the mixture is well mixed and creamy.

Divide the mixture among the paper cases and bake for 10 minutes until springy when pressed. If they have peaked in the middle, push down gently with your fingertips. Allow to cool in the tin.

To make the caramel filling, heat the butter and sugar in a heavy, non-stick pan until the butter has melted and the sugar has dissolved. Add the condensed milk and bring slowly to the boil, stirring all the time. Reduce the heat and simmer very gently for 20 minutes, or until the mixture turns a dark caramel colour. Be patient and don't be tempted to increase the temperature as it burns really easily.

Just before serving, top each cake with sliced banana, crème fraîche or whipped cream and grated chocolate or chocolate curls.

Pistachio cupcakes with pistachio cream

This is a very rich, nutty cake mixture. Don't worry if the mixture rises up in the oven and then sinks leaving a dip in the middle; it's quite usual and will be disguised by the topping. If the cream is too rich for you, these cakes are also good topped with a dollop of crème fraîche and chocolate curls.

MAKES **16–20 REGULAR SIZE CAKES**
PREPARATION TIME: **45 MINUTES**
COOKING TIME: **19-22 MINUTES**
PHOTOGRAPH: **PAGE 133**

¾ cup (3½ oz/100 g) shelled pistachios
⅔ cup (5 oz/150 g) cup soft butter
⅔ cup (5 oz/150 g) superfine (berry) sugar
½ cup (2¾ oz/80 g) semolina
½ cup (2 oz/60 g) self-raising flour
½ teaspoon baking powder
2 eggs
coloured sugar, to decorate
FOR THE PISTACHIO CREAM
¼ cup (1¾ oz/50 g) superfine (berry) sugar
⅓ cup (1¾ oz/50 g) shelled pistachios
1¼ cups (10 fl oz/300 ml) heavy cream (35%)

Preheat the oven to 350°F (180°C/Gas 4) and put 10 regular paper cases into a 12-hole cupcake tin.

Crush the pistachios using a pestle and mortar, or chop finely by hand or in a food processor or spice mill.

Tip the crushed pistachios into a bowl with the butter, sugar, semolina, flour, baking powder and eggs and beat thoroughly for 2 minutes until mixed.

Divide the mixture among the paper cases, being careful not to overfill, and bake for 12–15 minutes until lightly browned. Remove the cakes from the tins and allow to cool on wire racks.

To make the cream, grind the pistachios to a paste in a coffee grinder. Dissolve the sugar in 50 ml/2 fl oz/ ¼ cup water in a small pan. When it is dissolved, bring to the boil and boil for 5 minutes. Cool, then mix with the pistachio paste.

Whip the cream until it stands in soft peaks then swirl with the pistachio mixture. Pile on top of the cakes and decorate with coloured sugar.

Espresso cupcakes

MAKES **12 MUFFIN SIZE CAKES**
PREPARATION TIME: **45 MINUTES**
COOKING TIME: **17-22 MINUTES**
PHOTOGRAPH: **PAGE 135**

⅔ cup (3½ oz/110 g) dark muscovado or dark
brown sugar
½ cup (3½ fl oz/100 ml) milk
¾ cup (6 fl oz/180 ml) espresso or strong black coffee
¾ oz (20 g) molasses
½ cup (7 oz/200 g) corn syrup
1⅔ cups (7½ oz/230 g) self-raising flour
1 teaspoon baking soda
1 egg
FOR THE COFFEE 7-MINUTE FROSTING
1 egg white
¾ cup (6 oz/175 g) superfine (berry) sugar
a pinch of salt
a pinch of cream of tartar
2 tablespoons coffee liqueur or strong coffee

Preheat the oven to 350°F (180°C/Gas 4) and put
12 paper muffin cases into a 12-hole muffin tin.

Put the sugar and milk in a pan and heat gently until
the sugar has dissolved. Add the coffee, molasses
and syrup and heat gently, stirring all the time until
everything is blended. Remove from the heat and
allow to cool slightly.

Sift together the flour and baking soda, then add the
melted mixture and the egg. Beat everything together,
then divide among the muffin cases. Bake for 10–15
minutes until slightly risen and springy when pressed.
Remove the cakes from the tin and allow to cool on
a wire rack.

To make the frosting, put all the ingredients in a bowl
and whisk together with a hand-held electric mixer.
Stand the bowl over a pan of simmering water and
whisk for 7 minutes until the mixture stands in soft
peaks. Swirl the frosting on top of the cakes.

Fresh fruit petits fours

MAKES **24 PETITS FOURS CAKES**
PREPARATION TIME: **45 MINUTES**
COOKING TIME: **10 MINUTES**
PHOTOGRAPH: **PAGES 136-137**

1 cup (4 oz/126 g) self-raising flour
½ cup (4 oz/126 g) superfine (berry) sugar
1 tsp baking powder
¼ cup (2 oz/60 g) butter
grated zest of 1 lemon
2 eggs
FOR THE ICING
3½ oz (100 g) full-fat cream cheese
1¼ cups (7 oz/200 g) icing sugar, sifted
a few drops of vanilla extract
a good selection of fresh seasonal berries and fruits
2 tablespoons apricot or raspberry jam, to glaze

Preheat the oven to 375°F (190°C/Gas 5) and put
24 paper petits fours cases into 2 x 12-hole mini
cupcake tins.

To make the cake mixture, put all the ingredients into
a bowl and beat with a wooden spoon until smooth.
Divide the mixture among the paper cases and bake for
10 minutes until well risen and springy when pressed.
Remove the cakes from the tin and allow to cool on a
wire rack.

To make the icing, put the cream cheese and a splash
of hot water in a bowl and beat until smooth. Add the
sugar and vanilla extract and mix well. Spread the icing
onto the cupcakes and decorate with fruits and berries,
piling them high. Brush with jam to glaze.

Strawberries and cream cupcakes

Mix a few redcurrants with the strawberries when in season.

MAKES **18 REGULAR CAKES**
PREPARATION TIME: **35 MINUTES + 30 MINUTES STANDING**
COOKING TIME: **15 MINUTES**
PHOTOGRAPH: **PAGES 140-141**

½ cup (3½ oz/100 g) soft butter
3½ oz (100 g) cream cheese
⅔ cup (5 oz/150 g) superfine (berry) sugar
2 eggs
½ teaspoon vanilla extract, or to taste
1 cup (5 oz/150 g) self-raising flour
FOR THE STRAWBERRIES IN SYRUP
5 oz (150 g) strawberries, quartered
2 teaspoons superfine (berry) sugar
splash of rose syrup
FOR THE MASCARPONE ICING
5 oz (150 g) mascarpone
2 tablespoons icing sugar
1 teaspoon vanilla extract
2 tablespoons heavy cream (35%)

Preheat the oven to 350°F (180°C/Gas 4) and put 18 regular paper cases into 2 x 12-hole cupcake tins.

Put the butter, cream cheese, sugar, eggs and vanilla extract in a bowl and beat with an electric mixer or hand-held electric mixer until very light and fluffy. Whisk in the flour.

Spoon into the paper cases and bake for 15 minutes until risen and springy. Remove the cakes from the tin and cool on a wire rack.

To make the strawberries in syrup, mix everything together, being careful not to bruise the strawberries. Allow to stand for 30 minutes.

To make the icing, put the ingredients in a bowl and beat together until fluffy. To serve, top each cake with a swirl of mascarpone icing and spoon the strawberries and syrup on top.

Chocolate shots

MAKES **24 PETIT FOUR SIZE CAKES**
PREPARATION TIME: **45 MINUTES**
COOKING TIME: **10-15 MINUTES**
PHOTOGRAPH: **PAGE 143**

¼ cup (1¾ oz/50 g) very soft butter
¼ cup (1¾ oz/50 g) superfine (berry) sugar
1 egg
⅓ cup (1¾ oz/50 g) self-raising flour
1 tablespoon cocoa powder
¼ cup (¾ oz/25 g) ground hazelnuts
½ teaspoon baking powder
1 tablespoon milk (optional)
FOR THE BRANDY GANACHE FILLING
3½ oz (100 g) white chocolate
¼ cup (1¾ oz/50 g) butter
2 tablespoons brandy
½ cup (4 fl oz/120 ml) heavy cream (35%)
food colouring, optional
something interesting of your choice, to decorate

Preheat the oven to 375°F (190°C/Gas 5) and put 24 petits fours paper cases into 2 x 12-hole mini cupcake tins.

Put the butter in a bowl and beat to make sure it is really soft. Add the superfine (berry) sugar, egg, flour, cocoa powder, ground hazelnuts and baking powder and continue to beat vigorously until the mixture is well mixed and creamy. Add the milk if necessary to make a soft dropping consistency.

Divide the mixture among the paper cases and bake for 5–10 minutes until springy to the touch. Remove the cakes from the tin and cool on a wire rack.

To make the ganache, put the chocolate, butter and brandy in a heatproof bowl. Stand the bowl over a pan of simmering water and stir until dissolved. Remove from the heat, then stir in the cream. Colour with food colouring if you like. Whisk until thick enough to pipe, then spoon into a piping bag and pipe on top of the sponge. Decorate with whatever takes your fancy.

Lime and vanilla syrup cakes

To remove the seeds from a vanilla pod, split lengthways with a small sharp knife and carefully scrape out the seeds.

MAKES **9 MUFFIN SIZE CAKES**
PREPARATION TIME: **35 MINUTES**
COOKING TIME: **20 MINUTES**
PHOTOGRAPH: **PAGE 149**

½ cup (4 oz/126 g) soft butter
¼ cup (1 oz/30 g) desiccated (dry unsweetened) coconut
½ cup (4 oz/126 g) superfine (berry) sugar
1 cup (4 oz/126 g) self-raising flour
1 teaspoon baking powder
2 eggs
zest and juice of 2 limes
lightly whipped cream, to serve
FOR THE LIME AND VANILLA SYRUP
½ cup (3½ oz/100 g) superfine (berry) sugar
seeds of 1 vanilla bean
zest and juice of 1 lime

Preheat the oven to 350°F (180°C/Gas 4) and put 9 paper muffin cases in a 12-hole muffin tin.

Put the butter in a bowl and beat to make sure it is really soft. Add the coconut, sugar, flour, baking powder, eggs and lime zest and juice and beat thoroughly until well mixed.

Spoon the mixture into the paper cases and bake for 15 minutes until well risen and springy to the touch. Remove the cakes from the tin and allow to cool on a wire rack.

To make the syrup, put the sugar along with ½ cup (3½ fl oz/100 ml) water in a small pan and heat until dissolved. Bring to the boil, then stir in the vanilla seeds and simmer for a minute. Remove from the heat and add the lime zest and juice.

To serve, top each cake with a dollop of cream and spoon over the syrup.

Icing and filling recipes

Glacé icing

If you are doing lots of different colours then this icing is best made in small batches as it sets fairly quickly. If you want to make a really large batch as I once did when organising a cake-decorating school at my daughter's school fair, decant it into a large plastic tub and cover the surface with clingfilm (plastic wrap). In the school fête situation, small surface lumps aren't a problem and can be stirred in.

MAKES **ENOUGH FOR 12 CUPCAKES**
PREPARATION TIME: **5 MINUTES**

1¼ cups (7 oz/200 g) icing sugar
colouring, flavouring extracts (optional)

Sift the sugar into a mixing bowl to remove any lumps and ensure lovely smooth icing. Gradually add about a tablespoon of warm water to ice the top of cakes and a little less for piping, and beat with a wooden spoon until smooth and glossy. Colour and flavour as you wish.

NOTE: Accepted wisdom is that it's best to add small amounts of colouring gradually as soft pale icing is generally more appetising to most people, but sometimes bright garish colours fit the bill (and bright day glow pink with disco glitter is very popular in my house) – go with how you are feeling and dressing that day.

ORANGE, LEMON OR LIME GLACÉ ICING
Flavour with the grated rind and use the juice of the appropriate fruit to mix.

ROSE OR ORANGE BLOSSOM GLACÉ ICING
Use rosewater or orange blossom water in place of the water.

COFFEE GLACÉ ICING
Dissolve 2 teaspoons instant espresso coffee in the warm water.

CHOCOLATE GLACÉ ICING
Sift 1 heaping tablespoon cocoa powder into a bowl and blend with the water to make a paste. Stir into the icing. Add grated orange rind to make chocolate orange glacé icing.

FONDANT ICING
Fondant icing is easy to make at home with fondant icing sugar. It makes an icing very similar to glacé icing, but it stays soft and glossy even when set. It can be coloured and flavoured as glacé icing (see above).

Fondant modelling icing is made with the same sugar and less water to make a pastry-like dough that can be rolled out and used to cover cupcakes, or cut and moulded into decorative shapes. Ready-rolled white and coloured fondant icing is also available.

To colour fondant modelling icing, simply knead the fondant with your hands until pliable, then add a small amount of paste colouring and knead into the fondant until it is evenly coloured. Roll out on a smooth surface dusted with icing sugar or between two sheets of non-stick baking parchment.

Vanilla buttercream

Buttercream is my family's all-time favourite cupcake topping. It's a simple, versatile mixture that can be coloured and flavoured in many different ways. This quantity will make enough to cover 12 cupcakes with a good dollop.

MAKES **12 CUPCAKES**
PREPARATION TIME: **10 MINUTES**

½ cup (3½ oz/100 g) soft unsalted butter
1¼ cups (7 oz/200 g) icing sugar
1 teaspoon vanilla extract, or to taste
splash of milk (optional)

Put the butter into a mixing bowl and beat with a wooden spoon until it is really soft. Sift in the icing sugar and beat together until very light and fluffy. Add vanilla extract to taste. Add a splash of milk or warm water to make a softer consistency, if you prefer.

To make coloured icing add the colouring at this stage. See note on glacé icing recipe (see left) about colouring icing.

MAKES **ENOUGH FOR 12 CUPCAKES**
PREPARATION TIME: **10 MINUTES**

CHOCOLATE BUTTERCREAM
Blend together 1–2 heaping tablespoons of cocoa powder with a tablespoon of hot water. Allow to cool slightly, then beat into the buttercream.

TOASTED ALMOND BUTTERCREAM
Toast 2 tablespoons blanched almonds and chop finely. Add to the buttercream with a few drops of almond extract.

COFFEE BUTTERCREAM
Omit the vanilla flavouring. Dissolve 2–3 teaspoons of instant espresso coffee in 1 tablespoon of warm water. Allow to cool slightly, then beat into the buttercream.

FRESH BERRY BUTTERCREAM
Crush about 3½ oz (100 g) fresh strawberries, raspberries or blueberries and fold into the creamed butter mixture.

Raspberry sauce

This sauce is lovely with a warm chocolate cupcake and a scoop of ice cream.

MAKES **2/3 CUP (5 FL OZ/150 ML)**
PREPARATION TIME: **5 MINUTES**

7 oz (225 g) fresh raspberries
squeeze of lemon juice
splash of cassis (optional)
1 tablespoon icing sugar, or to taste

Push the raspberries through a sieve to remove the seeds. Add the lemon juice and a splash of cassis (if using) and sweeten to taste with icing sugar.

Hot chocolate sauce

Serve this sauce as it comes or flavoured with a splash of whisky, brandy, rum or your favourite liqueur. Using chilli chocolate gives it an unexpected twist.

MAKES **1 CUP (8 FL OZ/250 ML)**
PREPARATION TIME: **10 MINUTES**
COOKING TIME: **5 MINUTES**

7 oz (200 g) good-quality plain dark (semisweet) chocolate
¾ cup (7 fl oz/200 ml) heavy cream (35%)

Put the chocolate and cream in a heatproof bowl standing over a pan of simmering water and stir until the chocolate has melted and you have a gorgeous, glossy sauce. Serve warm.

NOTE: Any leftover sauce can be cooled, rolled into balls and made into chocolate truffles. Make a batch of mini muffins, top with a dollop of whipped cream and a truffle and serve with coffee after dinner.

Lemon curd

Fruit curds are easy to make but take lots of patient stirring and gentle heating to prevent the eggs scrambling. They're best made in small quantities and stored in the refrigerator.

MAKES **1 JAR**
PREPARATION TIME: **10 MINUTES**
COOKING TIME: **20 MINUTES**

zest of 4 unwaxed lemons
juice of 2 unwaxed lemons
2 eggs
¼ cup (1¾ oz/50 g) unsalted butter, cut into cubes
¾ cup (6 oz/176 g) superfine (berry) sugar

Put all the ingredients into the top of a double saucepan or in a heatproof glass bowl standing over a pan of simmering water and stir until the sugar has dissolved. Continue heating gently, stirring all the time – it can take as long as 20 minutes. It is ready when it just coats the back of a spoon. Don't let it boil or it will scramble.

Strain the mixture into a really clean glass jar (dishwasher clean is fine) and allow to cool before using. Store in the refrigerator.

VARIATION
Replace the lemon with 6 limes or ½ cup (3½ fl oz/100 ml) raspberry or strawberry purée.

Contents and index

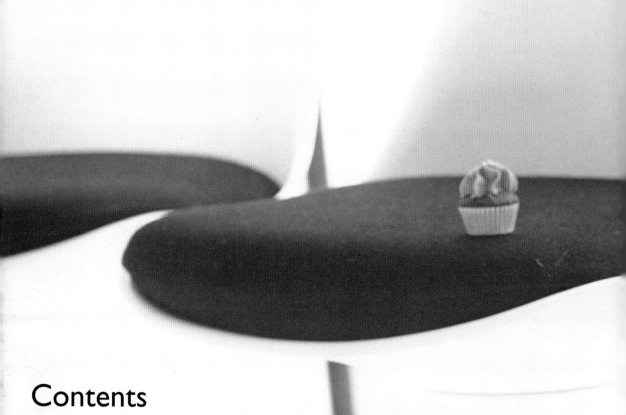

Contents

Index

Acknowledgments

Huge thanks must go to Catie for commissioning me to write this book. Thanks also to Deirdre – we made a great team and must celebrate with a glass of champagne very soon! Thanks to Kathy and Claire for their editorial patience, to Martin, Lesley and the Pomona Fine Foods team, to Gillian at Judith Michael & Daughter, and to Nadine for her knitting skills, not forgetting Ally B, who is a constant source of inspiration. Thanks too to Fiona, a talented nutritionist, for her original ideas – I love your version of gin and tonic with vitamins.

I would like to thank my family and all my friends, close and not so close, and send special thanks to Cas, Oli, Josh, Luke and Rose, and to Riley and family. A big thank you to Rick, Elliot, and Holly for their support and their talent as cupcake tasters. You are wonderful.

I dedicate this book to my mother who passed on her love of cooking to me. I would have loved her to share this moment with me.

English translation by Florence Raffy

This edition published in North America in 2009 by Whitecap Books Ltd. For more information, contact Whitecap Books, 351 Lynn Avenue, North Vancouver, British Columbia, Canada V7J 2C4. Visit our website at www.whitecap.ca.

All rights reserved. No part of this publication may be reproduced, stored in a retrieval system or transmitted in any form or by any means, electronic, mechanical, photocopying, recording or otherwise, without the prior written permission of the publisher.

The information in this book is true and complete to the best of the author's knowledge. All recommendations are made without guarantee on the part of the author or Whitecap Books Ltd. The author and publisher disclaim any liability in connection with the use of this information.

ISBN 10: 1-55285-963-0
ISBN 13: 978-1-55285-963-6

Printed in China

09 10 11 12 13 5 4 3 2 1